Penguin Handbooks
The Beginner's Cookery Book

Betty Falk was educated at the North London
Collegiate School and in Paris. She married
shortly before the war and lived in Brussels until
the invasion of Belgium. She writes that she has
travelled a good deal, collecting recipes en
route, is a self-taught cook and does not take it
all too seriously. Mrs Falk has two children and
one grandchild, enjoys gardening, lives in Reigate
and has a house in Provence. She has published
articles and stories and edited *The Shelter
Cookery Book* for Penguins.

Presented to
Deborah Higgins
for her poster entry
in the 'Bookworm Competition'
December 16th 1976

The Beginner's Cookery Book

Betty Falk

Illustrated by Judith Lamb

Penguin Books

Penguin Books Ltd, Harmondsworth,
Middlesex, England
Penguin Books Inc., 7110 Ambassador Road,
Baltimore, Maryland 21207, U.S.A.
Penguin Books Australia Ltd, Ringwood,
Victoria, Australia
Penguin Books Canada Ltd,
41 Steelcase Road West, Markham, Ontario, Canada

First published as *The Peacock Cookery Book* 1964
Revised edition published in Penguin Books 1973
Reprinted 1974

Copyright © Betty Falk 1964, 1973

Made and printed in Great Britain by
Cox & Wyman Ltd, London, Reading and Fakenham
Set in Monotype Baskerville

Contents

Acknowledgement

*My thanks are due to
Mrs Rosemary Johnson for her helpful
comments on these recipes.*
B.F.

Food and Drink

Why has our poetry eschewed
The rapture and response of food?
What hymns are sung, what praises said
For home-made miracles of bread?
Since what we love has always found
Expression in enduring sound,
Music and verse should be competing
To match the transient joy of eating.
There should be present in our songs
As many tastes as there are tongues;
There should be humbly celebrated
One passion that is never sated.
Let us begin it with the first
Distinction of a conscious thirst
When the collusion of the vine
Uplifted water into wine.

Let us give thanks before we turn
To other things of less concern
For all the poetry of the table:
Clams that parade their silent fable,
Lobsters that have a rock for stable,
Red-faced tomatoes ample as
A countryman's full-bosomed lass;
Plain-spoken turnips; honest beets;
The carnal gusto of red meats;
The insipidity of lamb;
The wood-fire pungence of smoked ham;
Young veal that's smooth as natural silk;
The lavish motherliness of milk;
Parsley and lemon-butter that add
Spring sweetness unto river shad,
Thin flakes of halibut and cod,
Pickerel, flounder, snapper, scrod,
And every fish whose veins may be
Charged with the secrets of the sea;

Sweet-sour carp, beloved by Jews;
Pot-luck simplicity of stews;
Crabs, juiciest of Nature's jokes;
The deep reserve of artichokes;
Mushrooms, whose taste is texture, loath
To tell of their mysterious growth;
Quick, mealy comfort glowing in
A baked potato's crackled skin;
The morning promise, hailed by man,
Of bacon crisping in the pan;
The sage compound of *Hasenpfeffer*
With dumplings born of flour and zephyr;
Spinach, whose spirit is the soil;
Anchovies glorified in oil;
The slow-gold nectar maples yield;
Pale honey tasting of the field
Where every clover is Hymettus;
The cooling sanity of lettuce
And every other herbal green
Whose touch is calm, whose heart is clean;
Succulent bean-sprouts, bamboo-shoots;
The sapid catalogue of fruits:
Plebeian apple, caustic grape,
Quinces that have no gift for shape,
Dull plums that mind their own affairs,
Incurably bland and blunted pears,
Fantastic passion-fruit, frank lemons
With acid tongues as sharp as women's,
Exotic loquats, sly persimmons,
White currants, amber-fleshed sultanas
(Miniature and sweetened mannas),
Expansive peaches, suave bananas,
Oranges ripening in crates,
Tight-bodied figs, sun-wrinkled dates,
Melons that have their own vagaries;
The bright astringency of berries;
Crêpe-satin luxury of cream;
Wedding-cake that fulfils the dream;
Pepper, whose satire stings and cuts;
Raw liberality of nuts;
Sauces of complex mysteries;
Proverbial parsnips, muscular cheese;

Innocent eggs that scorn disguises;
Languid molasses; burning spices
In kitchen-oracles to Isis;
Thick sauerkraut's fat-bellied savour;
Anything with a chocolate flavour;
Large generosity of pies;
Hot puddings bursting to surprise;
The smug monotony of rice;
Raisins that doze in cinnamon buns;
Kentucky biscuits, Scottish scones;
Falstaffian tarts that mock the chaste
Rose-elegance of almond paste;
Venison steaks that smack of cloisters;
Goose-liver for the soul that roisters;
Reticent prawn, Lucullan oysters;
Sausages, fragrant link on link;
The vast ambrosias of drink:
Tea, that domestic mandarin;
Bucolic cider, loose-lipped gin;
Coffee, extract of common sense,
Purgative of the night's pretence;
Cocoa's prim nursery; the male
Companionship of crusty ale;
Cognac as oily as a ferret;
The faintly iron thrust of claret;
Episcopal port, aged and austere;
Rebellious must of grape; the clear,
Bluff confraternity of beer –

All these are good, all are a part
Of man's imperative needs that start
Not in the palate but the heart.
Thus fat and fibre, root and leaf
Become quick fuel and slow grief.
These, through the chemistry of blood,
Sustain his hungering manhood,
Fulfilling passion, ripening pain,
Steel in his bone, fire at his brain . . .
So until man abjures the meats,
Terrestrial and impermanent sweets,
Growing beyond the things he eats,
Let us be thankful for the good

Beauty and benison of food,
Let us join chiming vowel with vowel
To rhapsodize fish, flesh, and fowl,
And let us thank God in our songs
There are as many tastes as tongues.

LOUIS UNTERMEYER

Introduction

This book in its first form was written for young people in their teens who enjoyed cooking and wanted to launch out a little beyond the bacon-and-eggs and fairy-cakes stage. However, it turned out to be found very often in the hands of new housewives, students and people of all ages and both sexes, some of whom had been cooking rather timidly for years, who were daunted by advanced cookery books and had never really got the hang of how to make white sauce without lumps.

It seemed to fill a gap left by all the books addressed either to dedicated and experienced cooks or to beginners who wished to work laboriously and thoroughly through the grammar of cooking to the *cordon bleu* stage.

It was therefore decided to revise the book and bring it out in a version intended specifically for the kind of beginner who isn't all that keen about spending his or her life toiling over a hot stove but seriously wishes to make a good job of the meals he or she chooses or is obliged to cook for family or guests, and without too much fuss.

The book will not tell anyone how to cook everything. Its aim is to enable the attentive reader to cook a limited number of interesting dishes well. Some of the recipes are very simple, some less so. A few are marked MORE ADVANCED. If they are long, it does not necessarily mean that they are complicated, but simply that it is impossible to explain them both briefly and in detail.

Basic techniques mentioned, such as making breadcrumbs (baffling, if you have never seen it done) or separating yolk from white of egg, are printed in small capitals and fully explained in the glossary. Words and expressions which are capable of varying interpretations (a 'large' onion, a 'clove' of garlic) are also in small capitals. If they are understood, it is obviously unnecessary to waste time looking them up. If, however, the beginner is in any doubt as to when an onion is large or what 'correct seasoning' really means, the glossary will explain.

For the benefit of those who have literally never boiled an egg, one or two absolutely basic subjects have been included, e.g. how to scramble eggs or cook sausages and mash.

The secret of using any cookery book successfully is to read right through a recipe before beginning work, to ensure that the general idea and sequence of operations has been understood and all the necessary tools and ingredients are to hand. There is no magic about good cooking; it demands common sense, concentration, a modicum of enthusiasm and a dash of imagination. This book enables you to do without the last, since ingredients and quantities required are stated as exactly as possible. Exact amounts of seasonings, however, are not specified; it is essential for a cook to train and learn to rely on his or her own palate and perhaps the most important instruction in any recipe is 'taste for seasoning'. If you should sometimes feel a compulsion to throw in a leaf of rosemary from the garden or a handful of raisins or some rather more exotic addition to a recipe simply because your sense of taste, smell or what might be called 'tongue touch' (the importance of texture in food cannot be exaggerated) suggests to you that this would be an improvement; and always supposing that the result is not usually disastrous, then you might be a very good cook in the making. Experiment and improvisation are the keys to inspired cookery. They can also produce some very nasty results indeed if the cook has no flair.

All the ingredients used in these recipes are easily obtainable in any town, though perhaps not in every village. Some are, of course, seasonal. I have not touched at all on frozen foods, which, though convenient, should in my view be used only in emergencies or when time is simply not available to prepare fresh food. Tinned fruit and vegetables are also, of course, a great facility, and soups in particular, especially if tarted up a little with milk or cream or chopped fresh herbs, are invaluable at times. But there is nothing as good, to my way of thinking, as dishes made from absolutely fresh materials.

Concerning parties, it is wise to remember that you are most likely to cook successfully something which you have already cooked at least once before so that you will not encounter unforeseen snags reducing you to a condition of gibbering panic half an hour before the guests arrive.

I have assumed that you have in your kitchen only the simplest of equipment. If you are fortunate enough to have labour- and time-saving devices and gadgets, so much the better for you; you don't need to be told to use a parsley-mincer if you have one, instead of a knife and chopping board. I have, however, referred in several recipes to an electric liquidizer. This tool, though not essential, is so useful in the kitchen that I would recommend anyone who can scrape the necessary few pounds together to invest in one.

I am not an advocate of the piping and colouring mania as demonstrated in the cookery illustrations of some magazines and commercial leaflets; who has the time, anyway, to pipe curlicues of mashed potatoes round cod cutlets for six? And the current trend, even in good restaurants, and even – may they be forgiven – in France, for decorating everything edible with pieces of tomato and a limp lettuce leaf is entirely deplorable. But neat, attractive arrangement of the food with no pools of grease and with a little sprig of parsley or a celery leaf makes all the difference to the appetizing appearance of the dish.

If you look around at your circle of acquaintances, you may be struck by the fact that there is a great deal of truth in the adage: *you are what you eat*. And not only *what* but *how*. I believe there is a strong connection between people's attitudes to food and their attitudes to life in general. You might care to play around with that idea while you pour half a bottle of rich, brown ale into the carbonnades flamandes.

Useful Information

Ovens

When using the oven, set it to the heat you will require at least 10 mins. (15 mins. in the case of an electric oven) before putting anything in. Milk puddings may be put into a cold oven.

You will find considerable differences in the assessment of oven heats among electricity and gas companies and writers on cookery, and even more differences between the performances of various cookers. The heats given in these recipes are approximate, and 10° here or there will not matter. You must get to know your own cooker and use the following table only as a guide.

	Thermostat setting	Approx. temperature centre oven
VERY SLOW	$\frac{1}{4}$	240° F.
	$\frac{1}{2}$	265° F.
	1	290° F.
SLOW	2	310° F.
WARM	3	335° F.
MODERATE	4	355° F.
	5	380° F.
FAIRLY HOT	6	400° F.
HOT	7	425° F.
	8	445° F.
VERY HOT	9	470° F.

The thermostat settings on old cookers are sometimes marked alphabetically. In this case, read approximately as follows:

A = 245° F.   D = 340° F.   F = 410° F.
B = 270° F.   E = 375° F.   G = 440° F.
C = 305° F.

Times

'Times required' given in these recipes are the overall times of preparation and cooking. They are on the long side to allow for inexperience, and actual cooking times are mentioned when relevant.

Measures

In the hope that you have the use of a pair of scales, which I believe to be essential to good cookery, quantities are given by weight. Some people use a British Standard measuring

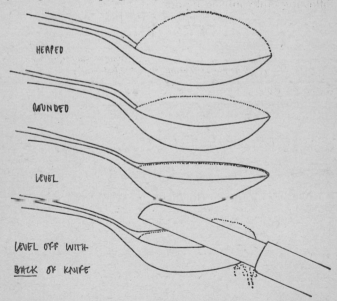

HEAPED

ROUNDED

LEVEL

LEVEL OFF WITH
BACK OF KNIFE

cup and set of spoons, which are satisfactory if you can get them.

When tea, dessert, or tablespoons are used as a measure, level spoons are usually intended and stated; if rounded or heaped spoonfuls are required, this is also clearly stated. You can level the contents of a spoon with a knife.

Flour	3 level tablesp.	=	1 oz.
Sugar	2 „ „	=	1 oz.
Rice	2 „ „	=	1 oz.

Butter is usually sold in 8 oz. packets. It is easy to estimate 1 oz. on a new packet.

LIQUIDS

4 gills = 1 pint (pt)
2 pints = 1 quart (qt)
A tumbler holds just under $\frac{1}{2}$ pt
A teacup holds just over $\frac{1}{4}$ pt

Spaghetti or other Pasta

Allow 3 oz. per head for a reasonable helping.

Rice

As an accompaniment, allow 2 rounded tablesp. (2 oz.) per head. (If there is some left over, it can be used in a salad.) If the rice is for a main dish, as for a risotto, allow 2 heaped tablesp. per head.

Parsley and Mint

The simplest way to wash these or other fresh herbs is to take the bunch by the stems, hold it under running water for a few moments, then give a few sharp shakes to throw off the water. It will then be dry enough to strip from the stems and chop.

Onions and Hands

There are various recommended methods of avoiding tears when cutting up onions. The only one I find in the least helpful is to stand near an open window. The peeling may easily be done under running cold or tepid water, which helps to prevent oniony hands.

Hands smelling of onion or garlic are not attractive even to yourself. I have actually been kept awake at night by the smell of my own hands and have had to stuff them under the pillow! To avoid this, either wear rubber gloves or use one of the special chopping gadgets on the market; or hold the onion or garlic with a fork in one hand while slicing with the other; but this is more difficult than it sounds. After peeling or cutting onions, always rinse your hands in *cold* water and rub with a little salt. If your hands do smell, try rubbing them with fresh parsley, crushing out the juice between your fingers, or with dry mustard, rinsing it off under cold water.

A piece of lemon rubbed over your hands after cleaning vegetables or washing up is the best possible way to whiten and soften them. When lemons are not available or are too dear, keep a small jar of citric acid crystals, obtainable from any chemist, handy. They serve the same purpose.

Meat

Don't put salt on steaks or chops before grilling – it makes the juices run out. Nick steaks once or twice round the edges with a sharp knife to prevent curling.

Kidneys

Don't put salt on kidneys until after they are cooked. It tends to toughen them.

Roast Potatoes

When roasting potatoes round the joint, you will get a crisper, crustier outside to them if you first put them into boiling water for 5 mins., then pour off the water, sprinkle the potatoes with salt and pepper, and shake them about in the saucepan to roughen up the surface. Then put them into the hot dripping, and baste them or turn them when you baste the joint. Finish them by themselves in an ovenware dish at the top of the oven, turned very high, if possible.

Butter or Margarine or Oil

Where butter is specified, margarine may be used unless otherwise stated, for reasons of economy or considerations of health, an excess of animal fats being considered by many doctors nowadays to be deleterious. The result, however, will not have the same blandness and depth of flavour. Also, margarine is more difficult for an inexperienced cook to handle successfully, except in baking. As to their relative food values, there is nothing to choose between them.

Vegetable oils are an excellent medium for deep or shallow frying of almost anything. For everyday use I would suggest sunflower or peanut oil. For some recipes of Mediterranean origin, olive oil, though expensive, is almost essential. A mixture of butter and olive oil is an excellent shallow-frying medium and the food is less likely to stick to the pan than if cooked in butter alone.

Serving

Always have hot dishes and plates ready for hot food.

Equivalent Measures

American Cup Measures

The instructions throughout this book are for the ingredients to be measured by weight. The table below shows some equivalent measures for people who are used to the American measuring cup.

It is important to remember that American and English cups are different sizes. The American cup holds 8 liquid ounces, while the English measuring cup holds 10 liquid ounces.

An American measuring cup takes:

Flour	4 oz.
Sugar (caster or gran.)	7½ oz.
Icing sugar	4½ oz.
Butter, lard, or margarine	8 oz.
Breadcrumbs (fresh)	1½ oz.
Breadcrumbs (dry)	3½ oz.
Grated cheese	4 oz.
Currants, sultanas, etc.	5 oz.
Syrup, honey, or treacle	11 oz.

Metric

1 pint	= approx. ½ litre
1 ounce (oz.)	= approx. 28 grammes
1 pound (lb.) = 16 oz.	= approx. 450 grammes

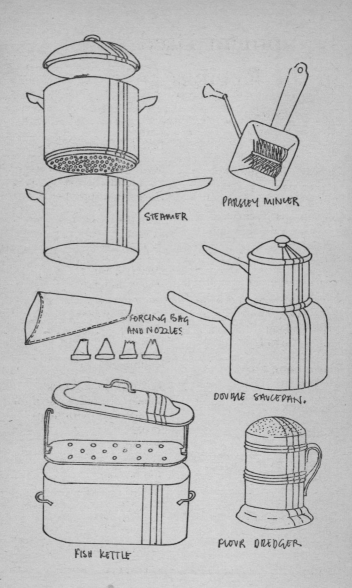

STEAMER

PARSLEY MINCER

FORCING BAG
AND NOZZLES

DOUBLE SAUCEPAN.

FISH KETTLE

FLOUR DREDGER

Equipment Used in the Recipes

Basic Equipment

Absorbent Paper
Aluminium Foil

Bain-marie or double
   saucepan
Baking sheet
Baking tins: various
Basins: small, medium,
   large
Bottles

Cake tin
Chopping knife and board
Colander
Cook's spoon
Cotton thread

Deep-frying pan
Dredger

Egg whisk

Fish-slice
Flan tins
Frying-pans
Funnel

Grater
Greaseproof paper

Jam jars

Kettle

Ladle
Lemon-squeezer

Measuring jug
Meat and vegetable knives
Muslin (for jelly-bag)

Ovenware casserole
Ovenware dishes

Palette knife or spatula
Pastry-brush
Pastry-cutters
Patty pans
Perforated spoon
Pie-dish
Pins

Rolling-pin

Salad spoon and fork
Saucepans; small, medium,
   and large (with lids)
Scales
Scissors
Skewers
Soufflé dish
Spoons, various
Strainer

Tin-opener

Vegetable-scrubbing brush

Wire trays

Desirable Equipment

Bean-slicer

Casserole to go on direct
heat as well as in oven

Deep-frying pan with chip
basket
Double saucepan or
porringer

Fish-kettle
Flour-dredger
Forcing-bag

Masher

Mixing bowl

Omelette-pan

Parsley-mincer
Pepper-mill
Plastic bowl-scraper
Potato-peeler
Preserving-pan
Potato-chipper

Saw-edged knife
Sieve
Steamer

Wooden cocktail-picks

Soups

Soups may be looked upon in two ways: as an introduction to a meal or, with the addition of bread, butter, and perhaps cheese and fruit or a salad, as a splendid meal in themselves.

A good cook can produce a creditable soup from almost anything – from a handful of stinging nettles to the fish bones she wouldn't dream of offering the cat – provided there are a few basic materials in the larder. The following recipes mostly require rather more in the way of ingredients, but you should find them easy and rewarding.

Half the value of a good soup is lost if it is not served really hot, so always heat the plates or bowls, and the soup TUREEN if you use one.

Watercress and Potato Soup

Watercress is a useful source of Vitamin A (necessary for children's satisfactory growth), Vitamin C (which, among other virtues, keeps the gums firm and pink), and also iron for blood – and vitality. As for potatoes, if you are worried about your weight, remember that white bread contains three times as much carbohydrate, weight for weight, as potatoes do, so it is more important to cut down on bread than on potatoes.

Ingredients (to serve 4–6)

1 lb. potatoes
1 small onion
1 or 2 bacon rinds (take these off the rashers with a pair of scissors)
½ oz. butter or margarine

¾ pt water
2 oz. watercress
Salt
Pepper
½–¾ pt milk

Utensils

1 medium pan with lid
Sieve or strainer
Wooden spoon

Knife
Medium basin
Chopping knife and board

Time required: 40–45 mins.

Method

1. Peel potatoes and slice coarsely, about ¼ in.
2. Peel onion and chop coarsely. A good way to do this is to hold the onion in one hand and, with a sharp knife in the other, score it deeply four or five times, first in one direction then in the other, then slice it across so that the onion falls in rough cubes. Repeat this until all the onion is chopped.
3. Thoroughly wash watercress. Discard any pieces of root or discoloured leaves, but retain as much of the stems as possible. Put aside about a quarter of the best leaves.

4. Melt butter or margarine in pan, add bacon rinds and chopped onion, and cook gently for 2 or 3 mins., stirring occasionally.

5. Put in potatoes, sprinkle with salt and pepper, and cook for another 2 mins., stirring occasionally.

6. Add water and cress, except the leaves you have put aside. Bring to the boil.

7. Cover the pan and SIMMER for about 20 mins., or until vegetables are soft.

8. Remove bacon rinds and pass the rest through sieve or strainer over basin with the help of wooden spoon, or use an electric liquidizer.

9. Return to pan, add most of milk, stir well, and bring to just below boiling point. Do not allow to boil again, as this changes the flavour of the milk and causes a skin to form, which is unappetizing. (However if it does boil, it is not a calamity.) Add rest of milk if soup is a little too thick.

10. CORRECT SEASONING.

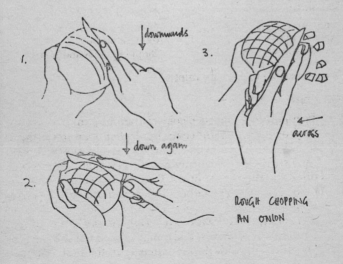

1. ↓downwards

2. ↓ down again

3. ← across

ROUGH CHOPPING
AN ONION

11. Last of all, chop the remaining watercress leaves fairly small, and add to soup just before serving.

CROÛTONS are good with this soup.

Minestrone

This is a soup to which you may add almost any vegetable or from which you may leave almost anything out, according to taste and season; but tomatoes and spaghetti must be included to make a true minestrone.

Ingredients (to serve 4 or 5)

1 large rasher of streaky or other lean bacon
1 CLOVE of garlic
1 large or 2 small onions
1 or 2 fresh cabbage leaves (not too large)
1 or 2 carrots (according to size)
1 small or ½ a large leek (when available)
A few beans, any kind
1 or 2 good stalks of celery (when available)

Half a dozen small sprigs of cauliflower or broccoli
A handful of peas (when available)
2 medium tomatoes, or half contents of a small tin of tomatoes
1 oz. spaghetti (or a little more)
Pepper and salt
1 oz. butter or 1 tablesp. olive oil or other good cooking oil

(If you have most or *all* of the above vegetables, which is unlikely, you will need rather more fat. You must use your own judgement; there must be sufficient to soften all the vegetables, but too much will make the soup greasy.)

1¾ pt STOCK if you have it (alternatively, the equivalent in meat-extract cubes)

BOUQUET GARNI

Utensils

1 medium saucepan
1 fairly large saucepan (with lid)

Spoon
Knife
Scissors

Time required: About 1 hr

Method

1. Cut bacon roughly into ½ in. squares with scissors.
2. Melt butter or heat oil in pan over low heat. Put in bacon and cook gently for a minute or two, stirring occasionally.
3. Peel onions and cut into six or eight pieces. Add to bacon. Peel garlic, cut into two or three, add to bacon.
4. Wash all other vegetables and cut into fairly large pieces, adding them to the rest in the pan as they are ready. Cut cabbage leaves into strips about ½ in. wide. Stir the contents of the pan often. Cook very gently for about 15 mins.
5. Meanwhile, heat stock (or dissolve meat cubes in water) and bring to boil. Add to the vegetables when they have cooked for 15 mins. Bring to the boil again, add salt and pepper and BOUQUET GARNI.
6. Add spaghetti, broken into pieces about 2 in. long.
7. Cover and cook gently for about half an hour, or until all vegetables and spaghetti are soft.
8. CORRECT SEASONING. Remove BOUQUET. Serve.

Grated cheese (preferably Parmesan, but any hard cheese will do) should always be handed round at table with this soup.

Artichoke Soup

Jerusalem artichokes, usually in the shops only for a short season, make a delicious, creamy soup.

Ingredients (to serve 4 or 5)

1½ lb. artichokes	¾ pt milk
1 onion	Pepper and salt
1 celery stalk	Few drops of lemon juice
1 oz. butter	Nutmeg
¾ pt water	

Utensils

1 medium basin	Knife
1 medium saucepan with lid	Strainer or sieve
Wooden spoon	Nutmeg-grater

Time required: About 1 hr.

Method

1. Squeeze a few drops of lemon juice into basin and fill it with cold water.

2. Wash and scrape artichokes (you may cut off some of the knobs to speed up this rather tedious business). Drop them into the basin of water: the lemon juice will preserve their white colour.

3. Peel onion and cut up roughly. Wash celery and cut into chunks. Then slice artichokes roughly.

4. Melt butter in pan over low heat. Put in all vegetables, and cook for about five minutes, turning constantly with the wooden spoon until all are well coated in butter.

5. Add pepper and salt and the water.

6. Cover pan and cook gently, stirring from time to time, for about ½–1 hr or until artichokes are tender (old ones will take longer than young ones).

7. Throw away lemon water. Rub soup through sieve over basin or use electric liquidizer.

8. Turn back into pan, reheat gently, add milk, stirring thoroughly so that soup becomes smooth and creamy.

9. Grate a very little nutmeg (two or three rubs of the nut against the grater) into soup.

10. Stir well, bring to boiling point, taste for SEASONING, and serve.

If you have one or two very young, pale green celery leaves, float them on top of the soup. CROÛTONS may be served with the soup.

Cream of Onion Soup

Ingredients (to serve 4)

About ¾ lb. onions
2 oz. butter or margarine
1½ level tablesp. flour

Salt and pepper
1 pt water
½ pt milk

Utensils

1 medium saucepan with lid
Wooden spoon

Knife

Time required: 30–40 mins.

Method

1. Peel and slice onions fairly thinly – about ¼ in. or less.

2. Melt butter or margarine in pan. It must not get hot enough to change colour, so keep heat low.

3. Put in onions and stir often, breaking them into rings with wooden spoon while they MELT rather than fry. They will soften and turn the colour of the butter after about 10 mins.

4. Sprinkle flour over onions, add a little salt and pepper, and stir again until the flour is absorbed and can no longer be seen.

5. Add the water, stir well, bring to boiling point.

6. Reduce heat, cover pan, and allow to SIMMER for 10–15 mins. or until onions are soft. Poke them with the spoon to make sure.

7. Now add milk, stirring as you pour. The soup should be of a thick, creamy consistency. Do not let it boil.

8. CORRECT SEASONING and serve.

NOTE: If you prefer a smoother soup, you can put all through a sieve or an electric liquidizer, and then reheat.

Cream of Tomato Soup

The sweet, red stuff sold in tins under the name of tomato soup or cream of tomato soup has little resemblance to real, freshly made tomato soup.

Ingredients (to serve 4–6)

1½ lb. tomatoes
1 large or 2 small onions
1 CLOVE OF GARLIC (optional)
1½ oz. butter (approx.)
1 teacup creamiest milk available
3 level teasp. cornflour
Salt, pepper

Bay-leaf
1 or 2 bacon rinds
Parsley, about 1 teasp. when finely chopped
Water, 1 teacup
Tiny pinch of bicarbonate of soda
Pinch of sugar (if liked)

Utensils

1 medium saucepan
Wooden spoon
Tablespoon
Teaspoon
Knife

Strainer or sieve
1 medium basin
1 small basin
Chopping knife and board

Time required: ¾–1 hr

Method

1. Wash tomatoes and cut (downwards) into several pieces.
2. Peel and slice onions (across) fairly finely; cut garlic into several pieces.
3. Melt butter over low heat, add bacon rinds, onions, and garlic and cook gently for about 4 mins., stirring often, until gold coloured.
4. Add tomatoes, bay-leaf, 1 teasp. salt, a good shake of pepper, teacup of warm water. Stir, and bring slowly to boiling point. Cover, and turn heat low. SIMMER about 30 mins. or until onions are soft.

5. Meanwhile, chop parsley. (This is also a good time to prepare the CROÛTONS; see below.)
6. Remove bacon rinds and bay-leaf. Pass soup through strainer or sieve over basin, pushing it through with a rotary movement of wooden spoon. Everything should go through except pips and skins of tomatoes. (Don't worry if a few pips do get through.) You now have a PURÉE.
7. Blend cornflour with a little of the milk and add with rest of milk to purée. Add tiny pinch of bicarbonate of soda to prevent curdling, which spoils appearance and texture of soup.
8. Return all to pan and bring to boil, stirring often. Cook very gently for 2 or 3 mins. CORRECT SEASONING (adding pinch of sugar if you like it).
9. Add chopped parsley, and serve.

This soup is improved by the addition at table of fried CROÛTONS. These must be made when the soup is nearly ready and served in a heated dish which can be handed round. (See CROÛTONS at the end of this section, p. 15.)

Egg and Oatmeal Soup or Speedy Soup

This rapidly made and nourishing soup is a wonderful stand-by on a cold evening, and with thick, fresh wholemeal bread and butter, a slab of good cheese, a tomato, and an apple is a perfect light meal at any time of day. To make it you need fine oatmeal flour – groats – sold at chemist or grocer as baby food. If there is no baby in the house, it is worth buying a packet and keeping it in the store cupboard. If there is some good STOCK in the larder on which to base your soup, so much the better, but good-quality chicken or beef soup cubes will do very well.

Ingredients (to serve 4)

1½ pts STOCK, or 2 soup
  cubes

3 level dessertsp. groats
1 egg

Utensils

1 medium saucepan
Wooden spoon

Fork
1 fairly large basin

Time required: About 5 mins.

Method

1. Heat STOCK (or dissolve soup cubes in 1½ pts water);
   bring to boiling point.

2. Put groats in bowl and press out any lumps with wooden
   spoon.

3. Break egg into groats, stir vigorously, and then beat with
   fork to produce creamy mixture.

4. Pour boiling stock steadily into bowl, stirring hard all
   the time.

Serve.

When possible, a little chopped parsley or CHIVES or watercress is an improvement.

Leek and Potato Soup

This soup, which the French call potage Bonne Femme, is
nicer served with CROÛTONS. Prepare these before the soup
is quite ready, and keep them hot in the oven. They must not
be put in the soup (or they will lose their crispness), but
handed round at table. Allow about a tablespoonful per head.
A little cream or top milk may be added to the soup just
before serving, to make it extra rich and delicious.

Ingredients (to serve 4)

About ½ lb. leeks (2 large or 4 small)
About 1 lb. potatoes
1 oz. butter
¼ pt milk
1¼ pts water
Salt and pepper

Utensils

1 medium saucepan with lid
Wooden spoon
Metal spoon
Knife
Medium basin
Strainer or sieve

Time required: About ¾ hr

Method

1. Trim and wash leeks thoroughly. Cut off as little as possible of the green. Slice them (about ½-in. pieces) and wash again in a colander under running water; there is often grit between the leaves.

2. Peel potatoes and cut into slices about ⅛ in. thick.

3. Melt butter in pan. Put in sliced leeks and potatoes, sprinkle with salt and pepper and cook gently, stirring often, for three or four minutes.

4. Remove from heat, add water, return to stove, and bring to boiling point.

5. Cover, and SIMMER until vegetables are quite soft – about 20 mins.

6. Either use an electric liquidizer or stand strainer or sieve over basin and pass soup through with aid of wooden spoon. All should go through. Use metal spoon to scrape last scraps from strainer. You now have a thickish PURÉE.

7. Pour PURÉE back into saucepan, add milk, and re-heat to just below boiling point. Do not allow to boil or the milk will make a skin and the flavour be impaired.

8. CORRECT SEASONING and serve.

T–B

Crème Vichyssoise (Iced Soup)

The Leek and Potato Soup recipe as p. 11, served ice cold, and with the addition before serving of about $\frac{1}{4}$ pt double cream, is the well-known American Vichyssoise. Sometimes a very few finely chopped chives are also added on top of the soup.

This soup is an unfailing success at any time of year when leeks are to be had. It is excellent as a first course at a dinner-party, enabling the hostess to concentrate on a hot main course.

Julienne Soup

This light and delicious soup can be made with almost any vegetables in season, but none should be too strongly flavoured. It is best when spring or early summer vegetables are obtainable. Keep the cabbage or mature turnip or elderly carrot for a MINESTRONE when you want your soup really to make a meal, or for chilly weather. A Julienne should be no more than a prelude to something more substantial.

If there is some good, clear STOCK in the larder, it will make a more nourishing soup than water and meat extract or soup cubes, but the latter will serve very well. It is difficult to give exact quantities of vegetables. Use your common sense and don't put in so many that they will clog the soup. The following is a suggested mixture. Vary or improve on it if you can.

Ingredients (to serve 4 or 5)

2 young carrots
1 small onion or SHALLOT or
  2 spring onions

1 very small, young turnip
  (or a piece of a larger one)
  no bigger than a golf ball

1 or 2 tablesp. young green
peas (after shelling)
1 or 2 French or runner or
GOLDEN BUTTER BEANS
1 or 2 stalks of celery heart
1 small tomato
2 cubes meat extract or clear
soup and 2 pts water *or*

2 pts good, clear stock
2 or 3 bacon rinds
1½ oz. butter
Salt
Pepper
Pinch of sugar
Mint
Parsley

Utensils

Vegetable scrubbing brush
1 fairly large saucepan with
lid
1 small saucepan

Knife
Chopping knife and board
Cook's spoon

A few asparagus tips if available (or even tinned ones)
add a touch of luxury, and a wine-glass of sherry – even
cheap 'cooking sherry' – put into the TUREEN at the last
minute is good.

Time required: About 1 hr

Method

1. Scrub or scrape carrots, slice rather fine, and cut into
   'matchsticks'. Peel onions and cut up small – they may
   be sliced finely and then quartered; spring onions may
   be cut into little circles or ½-in. lengths; turnip could be
   treated like the carrot or DICED; peas shelled, of course;
   French or runner beans must have strings removed and
   then be snapped or cut into small, chunky pieces; celery
   cut across into small sections; the tomato SKINNED and
   chopped. You should have about a cupful of neatly cut
   young vegetables – nothing much bigger than a new
   penny piece.
2. Melt butter in saucepan and SAUTÉ (lightly fry) bacon
   rinds and all vegetables except peas, turning them about
   in the butter on low heat for 2 or 3 mins.
3. Warm stock in small saucepan, or dissolve cubes in
   water, and add this to the vegetables together with a
   sprig of parsley and one of mint if you have them, and a
   pinch of sugar. (Leave pepper and salt until later.)

4. Bring to the boil and skim off any scum which may rise to the surface from dirt left on the vegetables.
5. Cover pan and cook gently for 10 mins. Then add any peas you are including, cover again, and continue to cook for another 20 mins. or until all vegetables are tender.
6. Remove rinds and herbs. CORRECT SEASONING and add salt and pepper as required.
7. Chop a little parsley and mint mixed – about a dessertsp. – and add to soup before serving.

Egg Lemon Soup

This is one way to make use of the carcase and trimmings of a chicken eaten the day before. It has a delicious, sharp taste to which people rapidly become addicted, and is very easy to make. It can also be served cold, as a summer soup.

Ingredients (to serve 4 or 5)

For the stock:

1 chicken carcase and left-over scraps, including skin
1 medium onion
1 or 2 sticks celery if available
1 small carrot
Bouquet garni
2 eggs
1¾ pts water

Juice of 1 or 2 lemons according to size
3 or 4 pepper corns, white or black
1 chicken soup cube
A little parsley
Salt

Utensils

1 medium pan with lid
1 medium basin
Lemon squeezer
Strainer

Wooden spoon
Fork
Ladle
Chopping knife and board

Time required

At least 2 hrs for stock to cook. It should then be left to cool and kept in refrigerator or coldest place overnight, or long

enough for fat to solidify on the top. To make the soup, about
10 mins.

Method

1. Make the stock: break up chicken carcase and put in
   saucepan. Peel onion, scrape carrot, scrub celery, cut all
   vegetables into pieces and add to carcase. Add the water
   and press bones down so that they are well covered. Add
   pepper corns and bouquet garni, bring slowly to the boil
   and simmer gently at least two hours. Strain into basin,
   cool, chill and when fat is solid, remove from top of stock.
   (Keep for frying croûtons, etc.)
2. Reheat stock which will have been considerably reduced,
   add soup cube and if necessary water to make it up to
   $1\frac{1}{2}$ pts.
3. Squeeze lemons and strain juice into basin.
4. Add eggs to lemon juice and beat lightly.
5. Chop parsley.
6. When stock is almost boiling (but not quite or eggs will
   cook) ladle a little out into egg and lemon mixture, stirring well.
7. Return all to pan and stir steadily over very low heat for
   a minute or two until soup thickens slightly and coats the
   back of the wooden spoon. Remove from heat at once
   when this point is reached. On no account allow soup to
   boil.
8. Taste for seasoning and add pepper and salt if required.
9. Add a little finely chopped parsley and serve.

NOTE: If you should have a disaster and there are pieces of
cooked egg in the soup, put it through a strainer. It will be a
little thin but edible.

Croûtons

These are small squares or cubes of toast or fried bread,
served with some soups and savoury dishes.

Fried Croûtons

Ingredients (to serve 4)

1 or 2 slices of stale bread
Dripping or butter

Utensils

Bread knife   Absorbent paper for
Frying-pan   draining
FISH-SLICE

Time required: About 5 mins.

Method

1. Remove crusts and cut bread into $\frac{1}{4}$–$\frac{1}{2}$ in. cubes. You need about 1 tablesp. per person.
2. Heat enough dripping in the pan to cover the bottom well, and when it is really hot (drop a crumb in – if it turns golden brown at once the heat is right; if it turns dark, the fat is too hot) put in the cubes and toss them about with the fish-slice until they are golden brown all over – 1 or 2 mins.
3. Turn on to absorbent paper for a few moments, then into hot dish, and serve as soon as possible.

Fish

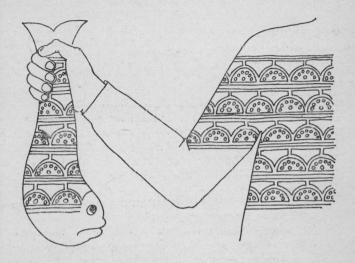

A culinary crime often committed in this country in restaurants as well as in the home, which ought to be punishable by a week's diet of cold porridge, is the serving of cabbage or Brussels sprouts with fish.

The only everyday vegetables which really associate well with fish are potatoes, boiled or sauté or chip (but never roast); tomatoes; and possibly sometimes fresh green peas or young spinach creamed. Small amounts of delicate vegetables, particularly mushrooms, and even fruit are often used in special dishes in fine cooking, but *never* a large helping of what we know as *greens*.

The flavours of fish are subtle and may be enhanced by a piquant or a rich, creamy sauce, but are totally extinguished by a strong flavour such as that of Brussels sprouts. By all means add to the food value of your meal by serving a salad or (as the French do) a vegetable afterwards as a separate course or before, as an HORS D'ŒUVRE.

Fish is a first-rate food, rich in protein. Some of the cheapest fish – herrings for instance (and that includes kippers, bloaters, and BUCKLING) and mackerel – are the most valuable, containing a great deal of oil (energy) as well as vitamins. So if you want a reputation for being economical, try to develop a passion for herrings.

Frying Fish

With certain exceptions, to fry fish in batter is in my opinion to smother both flavour and texture. It is much more appetizing fried in egg and breadcrumbs, or *à la meunière* (see p. 23). Small fish can be 'fried on the bone' or filleted; large fish can be cut in steaks or fillets.

Fillets of Plaice or Lemon Sole Fried in Egg and Breadcrumbs

Ingredients

2 fillets per person
1 egg (or more if necessary)
4–5 heaped tablesp. fine
  BREADCRUMBS, FRESH
  OR DRY

Flour
Salt and pepper
Groundnut or other frying oil
Lemon slices
Parsley

Utensils

Heavy frying-pan
Fish-slice
Knife
Fork
Clean cloth

Plate
Soup-plate or shallow dish
Sheet of paper
Absorbent paper for draining

Time required: About ½ hr, including making bread-crumbs, plus ¼ hr or more to *set* crumbs.

Method

1. Wash fish in cold water and dry well.
2. Beat egg in soup-plate.
3. Put breadcrumbs on sheet of paper, SEASONED FLOUR on plate.
4. Dip each fillet first in the flour, shaking off surplus, then in egg, then in crumbs, patting with knife to make them stick if necessary. Be sure to coat the fish well in each. Leave for at least 15 mins. for crumbs to *set*. Shake off any loose crumbs gently.
5. Put in pan oil you estimate will just cover fish. Heat until faint blue smoke rises.
6. Put in fish and fry until deep golden brown, about 3 mins. each side. Don't fry too many fillets at a time, or the oil will cool and soak into the fish. One of the objects of the coatings is to avoid this.
7. Drain on absorbent paper and serve garnished with lemon slices and parsley.

Cold Fried Fish

If fried in the Jewish way, this makes an excellent pre-pared supper served with salad and bread and butter, or potato salad. It can also be served hot this way.

Proceed exactly as above, but leave out the breadcrumbs. When you put the egged fish into the hot oil, the egg will form little curls and whiskers round the edges of the fish which you must scoop over the fish with a perforated spoon. If the fat is really hot, as it must be, they will be crisp and dry when the fish is cooked and drained, and will give it an attractive appearance as well as tasting good.

Halibut En Papillote

(Halibut in paper bag)
Paper-bag cookery is amusing and labour-saving and gives excellent results, and it has become easier since the introduction of aluminium foil, originally called silver paper, for kitchen use. Greaseproof paper can also be used, but it is more difficult to fold in such a way that the fish is really sealed inside.

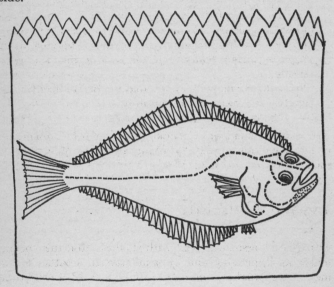

Ingredients

1 halibut steak per person, about 1 in. thick
1 oz. butter to each steak
Lemon juice

Salt
Pepper, black (fresh-ground if possible)

Utensils

Large sheet of aluminium foil   Clean cloth

Time required: About ½ hr

Method

1. Set oven to Hot, Mark 8, 445° F.
2. Rinse fish, and dry. Cut a piece of foil big enough to envelop fish completely, with a large margin; three steaks can go in one parcel, but if you are doing more than three, they will be more manageable in parcels of two.
3. Use some of the butter to grease the foil well, lay the fish on it, sprinkle each piece with salt, pepper, and about a dessertsp. lemon juice, dab the rest of the butter on top, then fold the foil over, pinching it together at the edges to form a sealed bag, but leaving plenty of room inside.
4. Place the envelope(s) on the middle shelf of the oven just as they are, and cook for 20 mins.

Serve in the envelope(s) on a large dish.

This is an excellent way to cook almost any fish. Try herrings or mackerel this way, but cooking for 10–15 mins. only, at medium heat.

Prawn Cocktail

YOGHOURT associates well with shellfish, and this cocktail makes an appetizing and unusual start to a rather formal meal. Don't make it too substantial – a little of everything should go a long way. If you prefer it, use mayonnaise and lemon juice in place of yoghourt and Worcester sauce.

Ingredients (to serve 4)

½ pt natural yoghourt (cartons are usually 5 fl. oz. or ¼ pt)

Pepper, freshly ground, black, if possible

½ pt prawns

½ lemon

2 or 3 drops Worcester sauce

A few crisp lettuce leaves

Utensils

Lemon-squeezer   Spoon
Basin   Knife

Time required: About 20–30 mins.

Method

1. Shell prawns (keeping four unshelled). To do this, hold the head and part of body firmly in one hand and three joints of tail in the other, and bend back slightly. Then pull off tail shell and draw body gently out.
2. Turn yoghourt into basin. Squeeze lemon and add juice to yoghourt. Add pepper and Worcester sauce.
3. Chop prawns into two or three pieces and add to other ingredients.
4. Wash lettuce, shake, and gently dab dry. Shred a little into each glass. Spoon mixture into glasses, adding a little shredded lettuce towards the top.
5. Garnish with an unshelled prawn on the edge of each glass or on top of the cocktail.

Serve, in small glasses or dishes, as cold as possible. Don't make it too long before needed or the lettuce will wilt.

Skate with Black-Butter Sauce

This is a classic French family dish (*raie au beurre noir*). The skate (which is closely related to the ray) is seldom seen whole. It is very large and singularly unattractive in appearance, with a long, powerful tail, beady eyes, and wing-like fins. Nevertheless, the flavour, particularly when boiled simply and served with black butter, is very fine. Never hesitate to buy it because it is a little unusual.

Ingredients (to serve 4)

4 pieces of skate weighing   3 oz. butter
    about ¾ lb. each   Parsley

Vinegar
Salt
2 or 3 teasp. CAPERS

Pepper, preferably black
(best of all freshly grated
from a pepper-mill)

Utensils

FISH-KETTLE or large pan,
preferably shallow
FISH-SLICE

Small pan
Chopping knife and board,
or parsley mincer

Time required: 15–20 mins.

Method

1. If using fish-kettle, place the pieces of fish on the removable strainer; if using pan, lay the pieces side by side. In either case, barely cover with cold water. Add a teasp. salt and a teasp. vinegar.
2. Bring fish gently to boil and POACH for about 10 mins. or until the fish comes away easily from the bone when a fork is gently inserted in the thickest part.
3. Chop parsley coarsely. You need two or three teasp. Have the butter ready in small pan.
4. When fish is cooked, lift strainer from fish-kettle, or use fish-slice to take from pan, and drain well. Place on hot dish. Scatter capers and chopped parsley over fish. Sprinkle a little pepper over or grind it fresh from pepper-mill. Keep hot.
5. Now melt butter in small pan and heat it gently until it begins to turn brown and smell nutty, which will be very quickly. Remove at once from heat at this point: although it is called 'black' butter, it must on no account *be* so. Add a tablesp. vinegar, swill it round the pan, and pour this sauce over the fish. Serve at once.

Sole Meunière

One of the nicest ways to cook flat white fish such as Dover sole, lemon sole, plaice. Very simple indeed. Known, for some mysterious reason, as *à la meunière* – literally 'the way the miller's wife cooks it'. Perhaps she ran a side-line in butter, for it is a method of frying in butter which preserves all the flavour of the fish – and in the case of Dover soles in particular it is almost a pity to use any more elaborate method. Fillets or whole fish can be cooked this way.

If you are cooking a whole fish 'on the bone', for each of four persons, remember that you will need an extremely large, solid frying-pan even to take two at a time, and to cook them in succession is going to make it rather a protracted business. If you don't possess a very large pan, it would be better to ask the fishmonger to fillet the fish. You can then get several fillets in the pan together and they will take less time to cook.

Sometimes you can obtain tiny soles, known as DABS or SLIPS, which are much cheaper than full-size fish and can also be cooked *à la meunière* and kept on the bone.

Ingredients

1 whole fish, or from 2–4 fillets, per person according to appetites	A little parsley
	1 lemon
	SEASONED FLOUR
About 2½ oz. butter per whole fish, or 2 oz. butter per four fillets, plus a little extra butter	

Utensils

1 large solid frying-pan	Large plate for flour
Fish-slice	Lemon-squeezer
Chopping knife and board, or parsley-mincer	Clean cloth

Time required: Whole fish, 10–15 mins. cooking time; fillets, 5–8 mins. cooking time; allow 10 mins. for preparation.

Method

1. Rinse fish under cold water and dry in clean cloth.

2. Put one or two tablesp. SEASONED FLOUR on plate, and roll fish in this until each fish (or each fillet) is covered.
3. Melt butter in pan; if you have more than one batch to do, do not use all butter at once, but add it as it is required. Get the butter hot; but it must not start to brown. Keep a close watch on the heat throughout cooking.
4. Shake the surplus flour from the fish as you pick it up, and place as many fish or fillets in the pan as will fit comfortably without crowding.
5. Cook one side for 5–8 mins.; then turn and cook other side for the same time. Exact timing is difficult to give. Test with the sharp point of a knife in the thickest part to see if the fish comes easily from the bone (or in the case of fillets whether it has lost its transparent look and is white and opaque right through). Fish should never be overcooked or it becomes tasteless and dry.
6. While fish is cooking, squeeze lemon and chop parsley.
7. Place cooked fish on hot dish without draining.
8. Now add a teasp. or so more butter to the hot pan, heat gently to a froth, add the juice of half a lemon (or whole lemon if you are cooking a lot of fish) and swill it round the pan.
9. Pour this liquor over the fish and sprinkle with one or two teasp. chopped parsley.

Scalloped Scallops

Scallops look rather like poached eggs lying in their fan-shaped shells on the fishmonger's slab. As with all shellfish, it is essential to be very fussy about their freshness. If they are in the least bit flabby or dull in colour, don't buy them. Unfortunately they are more often sold nowadays without their shells, pre-frozen, dull, unappetizing blobs for which I personally wouldn't give you the tail-end of a sardine. But if you can get them fresh, there are a number of ways of cooking them. One of the nicest is simply cooked in the shell, or scalloped.

Ingredients (to serve 4)

8 scallops with their shells	About 2 oz. fresh
Half a lemon	BREADCRUMBS
Cayenne pepper, salt	1 oz. butter
½ pt thick white sauce (see page 106)	A sprig of parsley

Utensils

1 small, thick saucepan	Baking sheet
Wooden spoon	Clean cloth
Tablespoon	

Time required: About 40 mins.

Method

1. Set oven to Moderate, Mark 4, 355° F.
2. Choose four of the deepest shells and scrub well. Dry, and grease with butter.

   NOTE: If the shells do not seem deep enough to contain two scallops and sauce, as is sometimes the case, you can discard them and cook the fish in any individual ovenware dishes, or all in one large, shallow dish. The only advantage of using the shells is that they look so attractive.
3. Rinse the scallops and cut off the BEARD, retaining the black, white, and orange parts. Pat them dry.
4. Make a thick white sauce.
5. Put two scallops in each shell, add a squeeze of lemon and a very little cayenne pepper. Cover with sauce. (Do not put too much in each shell – it will ooze out and be wasted.)
6. Sprinkle each with breadcrumbs, and put one or two small knobs of butter (about the size of a sixpence) on top.

7. Stand the shells on baking sheet and bake for 20 mins. in the middle of the oven.
8. Serve in the shells or ovenware dishes. Garnish with a tiny sprig of parsley on each.

Herrings à l'orange

Herrings are a splendid and cheap food, containing good supplies of protein, fat and vitamins; there is no better stand-by for the housekeeper who hasn't much money to spend on food. The most common ways to serve them are fried or grilled, with mustard sauce – and very good too. But there are lots of other ways to cook them. Try them with orange.

Ingredients

2 small herrings (or one large one) per person. (Get the fishmonger to split and fillet them, though it is easy to learn to do it yourself.)

1 medium orange to each 4 small or 2 large fish
1 clove to each small or 2 to each large fish

Utensils

Ovenware casserole with lid
Sharp knife or potato-peeler
Piece of greaseproof paper

Lemon-squeezer
Clean cloth

Time required: 20–30 mins. (according to size of fish)

Method

1. Set oven to Moderate, Mark 5, 380° F.
2. With knife or potato-peeler, take off one or two thin slivers of orange rind, avoiding the pith. Then squeeze juice.
3. Wash and dry herrings and lay each in turn flat in casserole; sprinkle with pepper, salt, cloves, and orange juice and fold together. Pour the rest of the orange juice over, and add the slivers of rind.

4. Cover with greaseproof paper and lid.
5. Cook for 20–30 mins.

Remove paper before serving and serve in casserole.

Finnan Haddock in Lemon-flavoured Sauce

Finnan haddock is the name given to the best whole-smoked haddock, and it can be distinguished from inferior kinds of cured fish by its honey colour. It may be poached in water or milk or a mixture of the two, or served in plain white sauce, but it is very much more delicious cooked as follows.

Ingredients (to serve 4)

1 large Finnan haddock (a
  fish weighing 1¼ lb. gives
  4 good helpings)
¾ pt white sauce (see p. 106)

1 lemon
1 thick slice of buttered toast
  per head
Pepper

If you buy a bigger fish to serve more people, make 1 pt of white sauce and use 2 lemons.

Utensils

1 large shallow saucepan or
  deep frying-pan, with lid
  to cover
2 small saucepans
Wooden spoon

Scissors or strong knife
Clean cloth
Lemon-squeezer
Strainer

Time required: About ½ hr

Method

1. Rinse fish and cut into number of portions required with scissors or knife. Dry in clean cloth.
2. Make white sauce and cook for 5 mins. only. Use no salt.
3. Squeeze lemon.

4. Remove sauce from heat; strain lemon juice into it, stirring constantly. Add pepper.

5. Place pieces of fish side by side in pan, pour sauce over. (If the thick pieces are not quite covered by the sauce, BASTE them once or twice during cooking.) Bring gently to boiling point, cover, and SIMMER for 10 mins.

6. Meanwhile, make thick slices of toast and keep hot. Butter these lavishly just before serving fish, so that toast appears to be oozing butter.

7. Serve fish straight on to plates, well coated with sauce. Serve toast separately on hot plate.

Garnish each piece of fish with small pieces of parsley or a celery leaf.

Cold Poached Mackerel

A mackerel straight from the sea, elegantly shaped and marked and shimmering with the violet and blue of the rainbow, is as beautiful as any dragon-fly; but you don't often see them like that at the fishmonger's. The colours of a mackerel fade quickly, but if it is really fresh it will have bright eyes, clear markings, and an attractive steely blue colour. If it is dull and looks soft and flaccid, don't buy it. This applies to all fish, but especially to mackerel, which deteriorates rapidly. Really fresh, it is a delicacy cooked in any way; served cold, with a good mayonnaise, it is as good as salmon, and much cheaper.

For this recipe, ask the fishmonger to clean the mackerel but not to remove the heads.

Ingredients

1 mackerel per person	1 teasp. vinegar
MAYONNAISE	BOUQUET GARNI
Salt	2 cloves
Peppercorns	Lemon
1 onion	Parsley

Utensils

FISH-KETTLE or large pan (a deep frying-pan will do) and a square of muslin or an old napkin

2 fish slices, or 1 and a PALETTE KNIFE
Large dish

Time required: 20–30 mins. to come to boil; thereafter small fish about 10 mins., larger ones up to 20 mins., plus 15 mins. for preparation and serving and at least 1 hr to get cold.

Method

1. Peel onion, divide in two, and stick 1 clove in each piece.
2. If using fish-kettle, place fish carefully side by side on removable drainer and just cover with warm water. If using pan, place muslin or napkin in pan, lay fish side by side on top of it, and just cover with warm water. The ends of the muslin or napkin can be folded loosely on top of the fish. Do not leave them hanging outside the pan.
3. Add the onion stuck with cloves, ½ teasp. salt, 6 peppercorns, the BOUQUET GARNI, and the vinegar.
4. Bring gently to boiling point and POACH for 10–20 mins. according to size of fish. Do not let water boil or all the flavour of the fish will be lost in the water and it will fall to pieces; it must gently SIMMER.
5. Meanwhile make MAYONNAISE (see p. 109).
6. See if fish is done by inserting a fork or pointed knife gently in the thickest part, near the bone. If the flesh comes away easily from the bone, the fish is cooked. Beware of overcooking.
7. If using fish-kettle, gently raise strainer, drain well, tipping from side to side, and stand strainer on dish; if using muslin, gather up the ends (you may need a fork to lift them from the hot water) and lift the fish as if in a hammock. Hold till all water has run off, then lower on to dish. Now, lift each fish carefully, using a fish-slice or palette knife at each end, and place on the individual plates. This is to avoid further handling and risk of breaking the fish.

8. Allow to get really cold, and decorate with slices of
lemon and parsley. Serve mayonnaise separately.

Serve with potato salad or tomato salad or both.

NOTE: You can, if you must, use bottled mayonnaise; but
beware – most commercial mayonnaise is heavily sweetened,
and ruinous to good food. By paying a little more you can
usually find good unsweetened bottled mayonnaise, sometimes made with lemon juice in place of vinegar.

Fish Cakes

There are various ways of making this old stand-by – which
can be an appetizing breakfast, lunch, or supper dish, or as
stodgy and dull as yesterday's suet pudding.

Ingredients (to make 9–10 medium-sized fish cakes)

1 lb. fresh haddock or cod
  fillet

A little over 1 lb. potatoes
  (they should weigh about
  1 lb. when cooked and
  mashed); you can use up
  cold ones if you have any
  left from previous day

1 small onion

1½ oz. butter or margarine

2 eggs

Salt

Pepper

Parsley

2–3 oz. stale cheese (you can
  leave this out if you wish,
  but it is an improvement)

3 or 4 tablesp. dried
  BREADCRUMBS

Oil for deep frying

Absorbent paper for draining

Utensils

Chopping knife and board

2 medium saucepans

1 small saucepan

Cheese-grater

Colander

FISH-SLICE

2 large plates

Soup-plate or shallow dish

Fork

MASHER (if you have one)

Deep frying-pan (with
  CHIP BASKET if available)

Time required: ¾–1 hr

Method

1. Peel potatoes, cut into thick slices. Heat some water in saucepan with a little salt, and when boiling, put in potatoes and cook until soft, about 10–15 mins.
2. Meanwhile, half-fill second saucepan with warm water and $\frac{1}{2}$ teasp. salt. Rinse fish under cold water, place in pan, bring gently to boil, and SIMMER for about 10 mins.
3. While fish and potatoes are cooking, peel and chop onion fairly fine. Chop parsley, about 2 teasp. Grate cheese.
4. Melt the butter in small saucepan, and very gently cook the onion, stirring constantly, for about 3 mins.
5. When the potatoes are soft, strain into colander, turn back into saucepan; add onion, with butter in which it was cooked.
6. Remove fish from water with FISH-SLICE, place on plate (tipping to drain off all water), flake fish from skin and bone with a fork or pointed knife. Add fish to potato and onion.
7. Break in one egg and mash everything together with MASHER or fork. Add cheese and parsley and a little salt and pepper. Mix all well together. Place mixture on floured surface and divide evenly into number of cakes required.
8. Form into balls with hands.
9. Beat the other egg in soup-plate or shallow dish with a pinch of salt and pepper. Put breadcrumbs on second plate. Roll each cake first in egg and then in crumbs, until completely coated. Flatten slightly with palm of hand.
10. DEEP FRY for two or three mins., until golden brown all over. (Beware of overheating oil.)
11. Drain on absorbent paper, and serve.

Serve with tomato sauce or CHEESE SAUCE (which should be made first and reheated when the fish cakes are ready) and watercress.

(Fish cakes can be prepared in advance and kept for frying when required.)

Eggs, Cheese, or Both

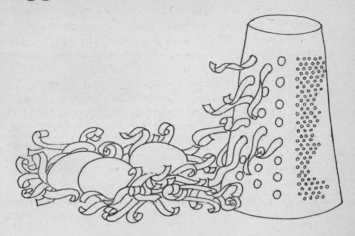

Important: When using eggs in cooking, it is wise to break each egg separately into a cup and make quite sure it is fresh before adding to others or to a mixture.

Omelettes

Someone who can make a really good omelette, even if he or she can't do anything else, is a person of considerable value. When there is absolutely nothing else in the house to eat, there will often be a few eggs, and a plain omelette, well made, is not to be despised. When filled with ham, bacon, herbs, mushrooms, shrimps, or any number of other things, it is a dish to equal any, and it has the tremendous asset of being very quickly made. It must, however, be eaten immediately. If there are several to be served, customary manners must be waived and as each omelette is ready it must be handed to its owner who must devour it forthwith. An omelette kept hot for more than a few moments soon resembles a damp wash-leather.

The beginner should not try to manage a large omelette. It is better to make a number of small ones, each using two eggs. As you become more expert, you can increase the number of eggs.

Any frying-pan *can* be used to make an omelette but a good cook will try to keep a shallow, rather heavy pan of medium size for omelettes only, and this pan will not be washed – only wiped clean with a cloth or soft paper. This ensures that the omelette will never stick to the pan, which it may do to one much scratched or roughened by scourers. If you do find your pan has morsels of egg baked hard on to it, warm it slightly and rub with a piece of soft paper, slightly greased, and a little salt.

If you have only one all-purpose frying-pan, don't be afraid to try an omelette, but keep your PALETTE KNIFE at the ready to slide underneath it, and use slightly more butter than you would otherwise do.

Study method well before beginning.

Ham Omelette

Ingredients (to serve 4)

8 fresh eggs (2 per omelette)	Salt
About 4 small slices of cooked ham	Pepper
	1–2 oz. butter
A little parsley or CHIVES	

Utensils

Omelette-pan or frying-pan	Spoon
1 small saucepan	4 small basins or large cups
1 PALETTE KNIFE	Chopping knife or board
Fork	Scissors (for CHIVES)

Time required: About $\frac{1}{2}$ to 1 min. to cook each omelette. In all about 15 mins.

Method

1. Break 2 eggs into each basin, season with a little salt and pepper, and beat just sufficiently to mix whites and yolks well, but not more. You can, of course, beat all the eggs together in one basin and divide the mixture into four as you cook it, but a beginner will find it much easier to keep each two eggs separate.

2. Chop ham into pieces about $\frac{1}{2}$ in. square. Chop parsley finely, or cut up CHIVES with scissors. Mix ham and herbs.

3. Warm ham and herbs in small saucepan with a scrap of butter, leaving the spoon handy ready to shovel some of the mixture into each omelette.

4. Melt sufficient butter in omelette-pan just to grease it really well (about a teaspoonful), swishing it round so that all sides of the pan are well oiled.

5. Turn up heat rather high, but not so high that you burn the butter. Immediately butter has ceased to foam, tip in your first two beaten eggs.

6. The eggs will at once start to set, and the whole operation must now be very swift if your omelette is to be light. Tilt the pan slightly, lifting the egg with your palette knife as it sets so that the unset part can run underneath. Continue to do this, running the knife all round the edges of the omelette and tilting first one way and then the other, until all the egg is set except the very top of the omelette.

7. Now put a spoonful of the warm ham and herb mixture on to this moist top, and with your palette knife fold first one and then the other side of the omelette over, enveloping the filling.

8. Slide omelette on to heated dinner-plate and serve at once. The outside should be barely tinged with brown and the inside still moist. The egg will go on setting in its own heat until eaten.

Don't be disappointed if your first omelette is not an unqualified success. You will improve with practice. Speed is the essence of it. Overcooking, which produces a dry, leathery omelette, is the most common fault.

(Under the heading Hot Puddings and Cold Sweets, on p. 119, you will find a recipe for making a soufflé omelette, which is a puffed-up version of the above, with a jam filling.)

Cheese Soufflé

'Soufflé' means 'blown', and lightness is the key word – it should puff up to twice its original size. There is a fiction that soufflés are difficult to make. In fact they are dead easy provided you stick to the rules.

A cheese soufflé can be served either as a first course or as a savoury, or even as a main lunch or supper dish. Once you have made one and discovered how easy it is, there are innumerable variations, both savoury and sweet, which a more advanced cookery book will suggest to you. A recipe for a chocolate soufflé is given in the Hot Puddings and Cold Sweets section, p. 117.

The essential thing to remember is that a soufflé, like time and tide, will wait for no man. It must be eaten straight from the oven or it will collapse like a punctured tyre – so arrange

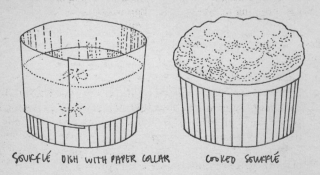

SOUFFLÉ DISH WITH PAPER COLLAR   COOKED SOUFFLÉ

your menu with this in mind. If you make it the first course and announce the meal to be ready when the soufflé is cooked you are pretty safe. Try not to open the oven until the soufflé is due to be ready; but if you must, open and close very gently, so as not to create a draught. Never open it for the first ten minutes, and *don't* try to cook something else at the same time.

Ingredients (to serve 4–6)

1 oz. butter
¾ oz. plain flour
¼ pt milk
3 oz. cheese (preferably Parmesan, which is expensive; but any hard cheese will do as long as it is not too fresh and moist)

4 eggs (i.e., 3 and 1 extra white)
Salt
Pepper
CAYENNE PEPPER
Butter for greasing

Utensils

SOUFFLÉ DISH, medium size (i.e., about 6-in. base)
NOTE: If you haven't one, a round, ovenware casserole would do or, at a pinch, a cake-tin, in which case have a clean napkin ready folded and a pin, and wrap quickly around tin before bringing to table.

2 medium basins
Small or medium saucepan
Wooden spoon
Tablespoon
Cup
Scissors
Pastry-brush
Pin
Greaseproof paper
Egg-whisk
Grater

Time required: ¾–1 hr

Method

1. Set oven to Fairly Hot, Mark 6, 400° F.
2. Melt a teasp. butter in saucepan and grease soufflé dish thoroughly, using pastry-brush. Cut strip of greaseproof paper long enough to go right round dish with slight overlap, and deep enough to come 2 in. above edge. Grease this thoroughly too, and pin it round the outside of dish (greased side inwards, of course).

3. Grate cheese finely.
4. Now make PANADA: melt butter in pan, stir in flour smoothly, cook for one or two mins. over low heat, stirring constantly, then gradually add milk, continuing to stir until mixture is thick and leaves sides of pan clean. Remove from heat.
5. Beat in grated cheese, a good pinch of salt, pepper, and a small pinch of CAYENNE.
6. Take 3 eggs and break one at a time, SEPARATING YOLKS FROM WHITES, into 2 basins. Add yolks to mixture, one at a time, beating each in thoroughly.
7. Break the fourth egg, setting yolk aside in cup and adding white to other whites. (The yolk can be kept covered in cool place and used for MAYONNAISE, custards, to add to mashed potato, etc.) Whisk up the four whites until stiff enough to stand alone.
8. FOLD stiff whites into mixture in saucepan, making sure to get your spoon right down to bottom of mixture.
9. Turn into prepared dish and bake for about 30 mins. Remove paper collar and serve at once.

You can bake this mixture in individual SOUFFLÉ DISHES or in paper cases. In this case, no paper collar is required, but fill the cases only three parts full and bake in a hotter oven for about 15 mins.

Egg and Cheese Fondue

A quick, light supper or lunch dish for two or four. It is not advisable to try to make this in large quantities.

Ingredients (to serve 4)

4 fresh eggs
2 oz. butter
3–4 oz. cheese (Gruyère or Cheddar)
A few drops Worcester sauce if liked

Salt, pepper (cayenne for preference)
4 anchovy fillets (optional)
Parsley

Utensils

Small basin	Wooden spoon
Small saucepan	Fork
Cheese-grater	Knife

Time required: $\frac{1}{4}$ hr

Method

1. Beat eggs in basin.
2. Grate cheese and add to eggs, with pinch of salt.
3. Cut butter into pieces about the size of a new penny and drop into mixture.
4. Put into saucepan and cook fairly fast, stirring often, for 4 or 5 mins.
5. When mixture begins to thicken, remove from heat and stir in Worcester sauce. Do not overcook. It should have the consistency of rather soft scrambled egg.
6. Serve at once in individual small dishes. Sprinkle each helping with a very little cayenne (or other) pepper and lay an anchovy fillet (if using them) across each.

Garnish with tiny sprigs of parsley and serve with hot buttered toast or rather thickly cut brown bread and butter.

Eggs Lorraine

This should really be done with Gruyère cheese, but a good imitation may be made more cheaply with Cheddar.

Ingredients (to serve 4)

4 thin slices of Gruyère or Cheddar cheese	8 thin rashers of bacon
	A little cream or top of milk
4 eggs	$\frac{1}{2}$ oz. butter

Utensils

Shallow fireproof dish, or preferably 4 individual ones	Frying-pan
	Scissors
	Spoon

Time required: About ½ hr

Method

1. Set oven to Moderate, Mark 4, 355° F.
2. Trim rinds and RUST from bacon. Heat frying-pan, put in rashers, and cook, turning once, until crisp.
3. Meanwhile, butter serving dish or individual dishes and lay slices of cheese in bottom.
4. Place cooked rashers on top of cheese, and break eggs carefully over rashers, keeping yolks intact.
5. Spoon a little cream or top of milk around edges of dish, about 1 tablesp. per egg. DOT each yolk with tiny piece of butter.
6. Bake until eggs are set, about 15 mins. Serve at once.

Stuffed Eggs

These always go well at a party as a buffet dish, or they make a pleasant lunch or supper with a salad.

Ingredients

1 egg per person (more if it is for a lunch or supper)
1 tin of anchovy fillets (this will be enough for 12 eggs)
Pepper

1 oz. butter
1 tablesp. lemon juice
A little parsley
A few lettuce leaves

Utensils

Medium saucepan
Chopping knife and board
Wooden spoon
Fork
Parsley-mincer (if available)

Teaspoon
Knife
Basin
Plate

Time required: About ½ hr

Method

1. Boil eggs hard – about 10 mins.
2. Put them into cold water, and shell immediately. (The shells come off much more cleanly before the eggs have cooled.)
3. Cut across into halves and scoop out the yolks.
4. Open tin of anchovies, and chop three fillets fairly fine. Chop parsley very fine – about 2 teasp.
5. Mix, in basin yolks of eggs, butter, chopped anchovies, and the oil from the anchovies. Add lemon juice and a little pepper. Mash all with a fork and beat to a smooth paste with wooden spoon.
6. Cut a fine sliver from the base of each egg white so that it will stand firmly on plate.
7. With teaspoon and fingers, mould the yolk mixture into the cavities in the whites. There should be as much above the cavity as inside it.
8. Cut the remaining anchovies into halves or into strips. Garnish each stuffed egg with one or two pieces of anchovy and a tiny sprig of parsley. Stand them on a bed of lettuce leaves.

You may stuff eggs with sardines, cheese, minced ham, or any other meat or fish, provided it has a strong flavour.

Hopla Popla

Rhinelanders call this peasant omelette *Hopla Pop* and a friend whom I taught to make it twenty years ago has spread it round the U.S.A. as *Hopple Popple*, but *Hopla Popla* seems to run off the tongue more easily, and this is how my family has always known it. The recipe varies from time to time, like the name.

Ingredients

About 1 lb. cold peeled cooked potatoes. If you are going to

cook the potatoes freshly, scrub them, cook them in

their skins in salted boiling
water with the lid on, and
allow to get cold, or nearly
so, before proceeding.
1 small onion
2 or 3 rashers bacon

6 eggs
Salt, pepper
About 2 oz. dripping or
   butter
Parsley or watercress

Utensils

2 frying-pans or 1 frying-pan
   and a shallow saucepan
Medium basin
Knife
Fork
PALETTE KNIFE

FISH-SLICE
Scissors
Perforated spoon
Plate
Chopping knife and board

Time required: About $\frac{1}{2}$ hr

Method

1. Peel onion and chop coarsely. Cut bacon into pieces about the size of a postage stamp or smaller, with scissors.
2. Beat eggs with pinch of salt and pepper.
3. Melt half the dripping or butter in frying-pan or shallow saucepan and fry onion very gently for 2 or 3 mins. Add bacon, and continue to cook gently for another 2 or 3 mins. Stir occasionally.
4. Meanwhile slice potatoes into rounds about $\frac{1}{4}$ in. thick.
5. Remove pan from heat, lift onion and bacon on to plate with perforated spoon, return pan to heat, add a little more fat, turn up heat, and fry potatoes until crisp and browned. Sprinkle cooked bacon and onion over potatoes and turn down heat to lowest possible.
6. At this point, turn on grill, ready for last operation.
7. Melt about 1 oz. fat in second frying-pan. When it is hot, pour in beaten eggs, which will start to set at once.
8. Now tip in hot potatoes, bacon, and onion, spreading them all over the surface of the omelette. Turn down heat a little. Slide palette knife underneath omelette all the way round, to ensure that it does not stick.

9. When most of the egg has set – about 1 min. – set the
   frying-pan under the hot grill for a few moments to set
   the top.

Lift the omelette from the pan with fish-slice and palette
knife and serve on heated plate. Serve garnished with parsley
or watercress.

Some people add coarsely grated cheese or chopped ham, or
both, to the beaten eggs instead of bacon.

If you wish to economize on the washing-up, you can pour
eggs over the bacon mixture in original pan, but your
omelette will take a little longer to set, with a risk of becoming
leathery.

Cheese Straws

These are excellent for any kind of party, and also as a
savoury course for lunch or dinner.

Ingredients (to make about 30 straws and 6 or 7 rings)

4 oz. plain flour	1 egg yolk
3 oz. cheese (Parmesan is best, but any strong, hard cheese will do)	Salt
	Pepper
	CAYENNE PEPPER
2 oz. butter or margarine	

Utensils

2 cups	2-in. pastry-cutter
1 medium basin	1¾-in. pastry-cutter
Sharp knife	Wire tray
Rolling-pin	SPATULA
Baking sheet	Grater

Time required: $\frac{1}{2}$–$\frac{3}{4}$ hr

Method

1. Set oven to Fairly Hot, Mark 6, 400° F.
2. Grate cheese finely.

T–C

3. Break egg, SEPARATING YOLK FROM WHITE in 2 cups. (Put white aside for other use.)

4. RUB FAT INTO FLOUR, add cheese, a pinch each of salt and pepper, and a good pinch of CAYENNE – but don't overdo it. The straws should have a bite to them, but not a choke.

5. Add yolk of egg and mix to a stiff paste with knife. Form into a ball with fingertips.

6. Roll out lightly on a floured surface to a strip about $2\frac{1}{2}$ in. wide and $\frac{1}{4}$ in. thick. You may find it easier to do this in two strips. Cut into strips about $\frac{1}{4}$ in. wide with knife.

7. When you have cut about 30 straws, form trimmings into a ball, roll out again $\frac{1}{4}$ in. thick and make 6 rings, using the larger cutter first and the smaller inside. It helps to dip the cutters into flour each time. With what remains of the pastry, make straws or rings, as you wish.

8. Place straws and rings on ungreased baking sheet and bake 15–20 mins., or until faintly gold-tinted. Remove with SPATULA and cool on wire tray.

Serve in 'bundles', with straws threaded through rings.

Tomato Cheese Spread

This makes a good snack spread on toast or bread and butter; or it can be used to make small savoury tartlets, using short-crust pastry. It will keep for several weeks in a refrigerator.

Ingredients (to make about 1 lb.)

1 small tin of tomatoes	1 egg
2 oz. fresh BREADCRUMBS	1 small onion
3 oz. cheese (Cheddar or Gruyère)	1 oz. butter or margarine
	Salt and pepper

Utensils

1 small saucepan	Wooden spoon
1 small basin	Grater
Chopping knife and board	1 or 2 small glass jars

Time required: About 20 mins.

Method

1. Peel and grate onion coarsely.
2. Make BREADCRUMBS. Grate cheese. Beat egg lightly in bowl.
3. Melt margarine or butter in pan and MELT onion for 3 or 4 mins.
4. Add tinned tomatoes, breadcrumbs, beaten egg, cheese. Stir well to mix, but do not allow to boil. Remove from heat as soon as all ingredients are well incorporated. Allow to cool a little.

Turn into small jars, and cover when cold.

Ham and Cottage-cheese Rolls

These are a good buffet-party dish. Made very tiny, they can also make part of a mixed hors d'œuvre to begin a formal meal.

Ingredients (to make 8–12 rolls)
½ lb. cooked ham *cut thin*
¼ lb. cottage- or curd-cheese

Utensils
Knife
Wooden cocktail picks

Time required: About 10 mins.

Method

1. Divide ham carefully into as many pieces as you require rolls, making all about the same size.
2. Put a little cheese on each piece and roll up neatly, pinning the roll with a wooden pick.

Arrange neatly in rows or a circle on dish or plate and garnish with parsley or watercress.

Croque-monsieur

I defy anyone to translate the name of this old French favourite. *Croquer* means to crunch. It makes a splendid and quickly made snack – but you must be sure to have a large, squarish piece of some hard cheese by you when you want to make it.

Ingredients (to serve 4)

4 slices of cheese, rather less than $\frac{1}{4}$ in. thick and roughly the same surface size as the bread

8 fairly thick slices of white bread
1 oz. dripping or butter

Utensils

Frying-pan
White cotton thread
Absorbent paper

Bread knife
FISH-SLICE
Knife

Time required: About $\frac{1}{4}$ hr

Method

1. Cut the crusts off the bread.

2. Trim the cheese so that it is a fraction smaller than the bread. Make four cheese sandwiches, and tie them together with cotton thread.

3. Get dripping fairly hot in pan, and fry sandwiches for two or three minutes each side, until outsides are golden brown and crisp and cheese is beginning to melt.

4. Lift out with fish-slice, drain on absorbent paper, and remove cotton before serving.

Decorate each one with a tiny sprig of parsley.

A variation of this is to cut the cheese rather thinner and put a slice of ham between two slices of cheese – and the bread outside, as before.

Eggs in Cheese Sauce

This dish is usually made with hard-boiled eggs, but can equally well be done with soft-boiled eggs, shelled and kept whole. In this case you will need a rather deeper fireproof dish, and you must make the cheese sauce before boiling the eggs and keep it hot until they are ready.

Ingredients

¼ pt cheese sauce (p. 107) for each 2 eggs. If you like, add a pinch of curry powder or of dry mustard to the sauce, mixing it with the flour.

2 eggs per person
A little extra grated cheese, about 1 heaped teasp. for 2 eggs

Utensils

1 saucepan (to boil eggs)
1 fireproof dish large enough to hold eggs when halved

Utensils for cheese sauce

Time required: 20 mins.

Method

1. Look up recipe for cheese sauce and gather utensils and ingredients required.
2. Boil eggs hard (10 mins. in boiling water) or soft (4 mins. in boiling water).
3. Meanwhile, make cheese sauce and keep hot.
4. Shell eggs, and cut in halves lengthwise. Place in fireproof dish (cut side upwards). Pour cheese sauce over.
5. Sprinkle grated cheese over top, and place under hot grill for one or two mins. to brown cheese.

Decorate with small sprig of parsley.

Egg and Bacon Pie

Ingredients (to serve 6)

6 oz. streaky bacon
4 eggs
2 or 3 firm tomatoes
1 very small onion
Salt
Pepper
White of egg (or milk) for
    glazing

For Pastry
14 oz. plain flour
2 oz. ground rice (or semolina)
2 teasp. baking power
4 oz. margarine
4 oz. lard
Pinch salt
About 2 tablesp. cold water

Utensils

Deep flan tin, or shallow,
    round ovenware dish
Large basin
Sieve or strainer
Rolling-pin

Scissors
Knife
Pastry-brush
Chopping knife and board
Clean cloth

Time required: About 1½ hrs

Method

1. Set oven to Fairly Hot, Mark 6, 400° F.
2. Make pastry. Sieve all dry ingredients into basin.
3. RUB in fats with fingertips until mixture resembles fine breadcrumbs.
4. Add 2 tablesp. cold water gradually, mixing with knife, until all flour is taken up. Form into ball of soft dough with fingertips.
5. Roll out lightly on lightly floured surface to about ¼ in. thick. Stand tin or dish on pastry and draw a line round outer edge with knife. Remove dish and cut pastry to line it, pressing pastry lightly but firmly down. Re-roll and cut slightly larger circle to form cover.
6. Cut rinds and RUST from bacon and cut rashers into about three pieces.

7. Peel and chop onion finely. Wash, dry, and slice tomatoes.
8. Line bottom of pie with bacon. Then add tomatoes and bacon, sprinkled with onion, in layers.
9. Break eggs over rest of ingredients, keeping them evenly spaced as far as possible. It is of no importance if the yolks break. Sprinkle with salt and pepper.
10. Lay pastry-cover on top, and knock up edges with back of knife, or FLUTE them. Cut leaves of pastry (elongated diamond shapes) from the trimmings and decorate the centre of the pie with them. Make a small hole in the centre with the point of a knife.
11. Brush pie with white of egg to glaze it.
12. Bake for ½ hr or a little longer, until golden brown and risen. The eggs should be set inside.

Serve hot or cold, decorated with sprigs of parsley.

Salads

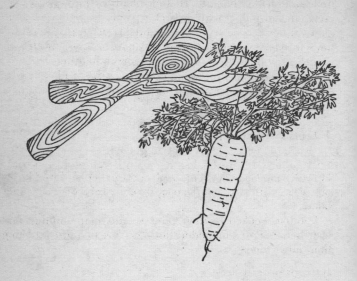

Salads can be served as a course, as a meal, or as an accompaniment to meat or PASTA. A steak or chicken accompanied by a simple green salad with a FRENCH DRESSING is a pleasant change from the usual 'and two veg', and is becoming increasingly popular.

Raw salads are a most valuable form of food, and the less you shred and chop them the less you will lose of their precious minerals and vitamins. So when you make a mixed salad, add small whole or halved carrots, sticks of tender celery, beetroots the size of golf-balls, spring onions, or any other whole vegetables you can think of. You can make salads with cooked vegetables too, of course, and provided you cook them quickly in very little boiling water (try to keep the water to add to soups or gravies) you won't lose too much of the food values.

A good mixed diet gives you most of the vitamins you need,

as long as it includes plenty of fresh vegetables and fruit. You can make salads with almost any edible plant. Let your imagination have full rein. Include plenty of tomatoes, watercress, mustard and cress, Brussels sprouts, as well as carrots, cabbage, lettuce, celery, young dandelion leaves, nuts, raisins and sultanas, apples, pimentoes, mushrooms, beetroots, onions, new potatoes, and so on almost indefinitely.

Salads look best in wooden or plain china or glass bowls. The following recipes are just to give you a few ideas.

Potato Salad

Potato salad is excellent with hot or cold Frankfurter sausages, with any cold meats or cold fish, or with other salads.

Potatoes cooked in their skins retain their vitamins and taste better. Eaten in moderation, they are no more fattening than other foods.

Ingredients (to serve 4)

1½ lb. potatoes (floury potatoes are not suitable, but new potatoes are excellent)	Pepper and salt
	A little CAYENNE PEPPER if available
¼ pt MAYONNAISE	Small piece of celery if available
1 spring onion, or a small piece of onion	Parsley

Utensils

Medium saucepan	Colander
Chopping knife and board	Clean cloth
Parsley-mincer, if available	Salad spoon and fork

Time required: This may vary from 20–40 mins. according to the size and type of potatoes being used. Add to this time for the salad to get really cold.

Method
  1. Scrub potatoes, but do not peel.

2. Put potatoes into a pan of boiling salted water. Boil gently for from 10 mins. in the case of small new potatoes to 30 mins. for large old ones. (The very large kinds are unlikely to be suitable for potato salad.) To see if they are done, plunge a skewer or pointed knife into the centre of one of the largest and feel whether it is soft all through.

3. While potatoes are cooking, peel and finely chop about a heaped teasp. of onion. Spring onion may be chopped fairly coarsely and the green part sliced, and more may be used, as it is milder. If you have any celery, chop this finely too, about a heaped teasp. Chop about the same amount of parsley.

4. Drain potatoes in colander; when cool enough to handle, skin them with a sharp knife, holding the hot potato in a clean cloth.

5. Cut them up. Small new potatoes may be simply sliced; large ones should be cut into cubes rather larger than a postage stamp.

6. When no longer hot but still warm, using salad spoon and fork (a metal spoon will break them up) mix in MAYONNAISE, chopped onion, celery if any, a little salt and pepper, and most of the parsley. Turn it all about until each piece of potato is well coated with the other ingredients, but be careful not to mash the potato. Taste, and CORRECT SEASONING.

7. Turn into clean, attractive dish or bowl, and sprinkle the rest of the parsley on top – and just a very few grains of CAYENNE PEPPER (which is infernally hot), mainly for its decorative effect.

8. Allow to get quite cold before serving; but it should *not* be chilled in the refrigerator.

Spanish Salad

If you want something substantial to go with cold meats of any kind, rice is a change from potato salad. It is good with

fish too. There are several simple operations required, which
makes the recipe appear long and complicated, but in fact all
are quickly and easily done. The salad can be made well in
advance, the day before it is needed if you like. It will keep
for several days.

Ingredients (to serve 6)

8 heaped tablesp. Patna rice
or other long-grain rice
2–3 oz. mushrooms (the
white ones)
½ oz. butter
¼–½ pimento (preferably
red; green or yellow will
do)
½ lemon
4 small firm tomatoes

A small piece of onion, or
1 spring onion
3 tablesp. olive oil
1½ tablesp. vinegar
Salt
Pepper (preferably black,
fresh-ground)
A few black or small green
olives (optional)

Utensils

Large saucepan
2 small saucepans
Cook's spoon
Fork
Strainer
Chopping board and knife
Plate

Kettle
Clean cloth
2 large basins and 1 small
Lemon-squeezer
Saw-edged or other slicing
knife

Time required: About ¾ hr to make, 1 hr at least to cool.

Method

1. Boil about 6 pts of water with 2 teasp. salt in large saucepan.

2. Rinse rice well in strainer under cold tap and then pour
it slowly into the boiling water. Boil fast until cooked –
about 20 mins. (Different rices take different times to
cook; test by biting a few grains.) Stir occasionally.

3. Put kettle of water on low heat, so that it is boiling by the
time rice is cooked.

4. Meanwhile, prepare pimento and mushrooms; wash

pimento, cut down centre, and remove pips and core. (Put away in larder or fridge the part that you are not using for this recipe; it can be used raw in salads or cooked in another dish.) Slice the piece you are using into $\frac{1}{2}$-in. strips.

5. Have water boiling in small pan, with $\frac{1}{2}$ teasp. salt. Put in pimento and cook till soft – 5–10 mins. Don't overcook. Drain well in strainer. Put on plate to cool.

6. Rinse mushrooms in strainer under cold tap (do not peel). Pat them dry and cut them into four or eight pieces according to size, including stalks.

7. Wash and chop onion finely.

8. Squeeze lemon.

9. Melt butter in small pan, put in lemon juice and chopped mushrooms, a little salt and pepper. Cook gently for 5–10 mins. until mushrooms are just soft. Put aside to cool.

10. By now, the rice is probably done. Kettle of water must be boiling. Strain rice over large bowl. Lift strainer, hold over sink, and pour boiling water slowly over rice to separate grains. Drain well and turn into another large bowl. Allow to cool, stirring occasionally with fork.

11. Slice tomatoes fairly fine.

12. When rice is nearly cold, add to it the cooked pimentoes, mushrooms in their liquor, onion, and olives if you are including them.

13. Make dressing of olive oil, vinegar, salt, and pepper in small bowl. Mix well and pour over rice, etc. Mix well, taste, and CORRECT SEASONING.

14. Add tomatoes last of all and mix in as gently as possible so as not to break them up. Turn all into clean wooden or other salad bowl.

Serve quite cold.

Green Bean Salad

This can be made in summer with fresh beans and in winter with frozen beans (prepared *exactly* as instructed on the packet if you don't want to lose all the vitamins) or tinned beans. There are some excellent, if rather expensive, Belgian tinned beans on the market, which make an almost better salad then fresh ones. If you have a garden, persuade whoever is responsible for the vegetables to grow GOLDEN BUTTER BEANS, a foolproof crop and delicious either hot or cold.

Ingredients (to serve 4)

2 lb. runner or French beans (or golden butter beans)
1 small CLOVE OF GARLIC, or a little GARLIC SALT
1 small tablesp. vinegar (preferably WINE VINEGAR)

2 tablesp. olive oil
Salt
Pepper (preferably black and fresh-ground)

Utensils

Large saucepan
Colander
Knife

Salad bowl
Salad spoon and fork
Wooden spoon

Time required: To prepare: Variable, depending on age of beans and your skill. To cook: About 10 mins.

Method

Exactly as recipe for Green Beans with Butter. Method, paras. 1–5 (p. 70).

6. Meanwhile, peel CLOVE OF GARLIC and crush it against side of salad bowl with wooden or salad spoon, rubbing it well all round the bowl. If you like a strong flavour of garlic, leave the pieces in the bowl; otherwise remove them, leaving just the oil of the garlic on the sides of the

bowl. If you use only GARLIC SALT, wait until you make the dressing, and use it in place of ordinary salt.

7. Put beans in bowl and leave until nearly cold.
8. Make dressing of oil, vinegar, a little (small half teasp.) salt and a little pepper. Pour over beans and toss them well in the dressing until all are coated with it. Taste, and CORRECT SEASONING.

Serve cold but not chilled.

Sliced tomatoes mixed with the beans make a very good alternative salad.

Tomato Salad

(Tomatoes are a very good source of Vitamin C.)

It is impossible to give exact quantities for this salad, as for many others. You must use your own discretion and put in as much onion and parsley as your taste dictates.

Ingredients

1, 2, or 3 firm ripe tomatoes per person according to size (the tomatoes, not the persons)

A small piece of onion, or a spring onion
Parsley
FRENCH DRESSING (see p. 112)

Utensils

A saw-edged knife, or a tomato-slicer or other sharp knife
Chopping knife and board

Parsley-mincer if you have one
Clean cloth

Time required: 10 mins. or a little longer to make; it is preferable to let the salad stand at least half an hour before serving.

Method

1. Wash and dry tomatoes, and slice rather thinly into salad bowl or dish.
2. Peel and chop onion finely and sprinkle over tomatoes. Spring onions can be sliced across thinly and the green part chopped into short lengths.
3. Chop parsley finely and sprinkle over tomatoes.
4. Make FRENCH DRESSING pour over salad, and turn the tomatoes gently in it, being careful not to break them up.

Any dressing left in the bowl after the salad has been eaten will be partly tomato juice and can be kept in a cool place until another tomato salad is wanted, or to dress a green salad. Alternatively, share it round and do as the French do with any sauce left over – mop it up with pieces of bread on the end of your fork.

Green Salad

Salad in this country nearly always means a mixture based on lettuce and including tomatoes, hard-boiled eggs, beet-roots, onions, and various other vegetables. This is very pleasant sometimes, but it is not really necessary to put every-thing but the kitchen stove in every time. On the Continent (and increasingly here too), a steak is served more often accompanied by a green salad than by cooked vegetables, as we usually serve it. Incidentally, steak with a green salad is a perfect meal for people who are trying to lose weight.

Lettuce may be used alone, or as the basis of a green salad, mixed with any kind of cress, chicory, endive, celery, young dandelion leaves from the garden, spring onions, and any other green salad stuff you are able to get hold of. All should be well washed, shaken dry in a SALAD SHAKER, and gently dabbed with a clean cloth to remove remaining water. *Never* cut lettuce with a knife; use the leaves whole if you can, or, if they are too large to be eaten conveniently with a fork, tear them with your fingers (when you make the salad – not at table).

A green salad should have a FRENCH DRESSING (p. 112), which may be varied by the use of different herb-flavoured vinegars, TARRAGON being the most common. If you like garlic, peel a CLOVE OF GARLIC, crush it in the salad bowl with the back of the salad spoon or a wooden spoon, and rub it well round the sides of the bowl. Discard the pieces – the oil on the bowl will be sufficient to flavour the salad. If you use garlic, you may leave out the onions in the salad.

The correct way to dress a green salad or any mixed salad is as follows. (Leave out beetroot, tomato, or egg which will spoil the appearance of the salad and should be added after the rest has been dressed.)

1. Put the washed and dried salad in the salad bowl (previously rubbed with garlic if you like).

2. Measure out the oil, and pour this on first. With the salad spoon and fork (if you are preparing a great deal of salad, say for a party, scrub your hands well and use them instead; it is quite the best way) turn the leaves about until every leaf is glistening with oil, before anything else is added.

3. Mix salt, pepper, and mustard if you are using it, in the salad spoon, and a little of the vinegar, stirring it with the fork. Pour this over the salad, and then the rest of the vinegar. Now mix it all thoroughly again, but as gently as possible, so as not to bruise the leaves.

Serve at once. A salad based on lettuce should never stand for more than a few minutes after it is dressed – otherwise the lettuce will 'fall', that is become sodden with the dressing instead of coated with it.

Alternatively, make a quantity of FRENCH DRESSING and keep it in a closed jar or bottle. This will be perfectly all right provided it is well shaken before use; it will keep indefinitely and is a great time-saver.

Mushroom Salad

If you have never eaten raw mushrooms, a delightful experience awaits you. This salad is good as part of a mixed HORS D'ŒUVRE but it is not to be eaten in vast quantities.

Ingredients

½ lb. white mushrooms, very fresh
1 tablesp. lemon juice
Pepper
Salt
A few CHIVES or a little parsley
About 4 tablesp. olive oil

Utensils

Bowl
Fork
Knife
Clean cloth

Time required: 10 mins. to prepare, 1½ hrs to stand

Method

1. Wash mushrooms and pat dry. (Do not peel.) Cut off most of stalk (and put aside to add to stews or stock). Slice the rest thinly, across the caps, and put in salad bowl.

2. Mix oil with lemon juice, salt and pepper, and beat well.

3. Pour about ⅔ of this dressing over mushrooms, stir, and put aside for an hour.

4. Add rest of dressing and allow to stand again until most of dressing is absorbed, about ½ hr.

5. Meanwhile, chop CHIVES or parsley; about 1 teasp. parsley will be enough, but rather more CHIVES may be used. Sprinkle this over salad, and serve.

A good, simple mixed hors d'œuvre to begin a formal meal might consist of mushroom salad, tomato salad, shrimps, olives, sardines, and some kind of pickled herring.

Cabbage Salad

This makes a useful alternative to the eternal lettuce; it is often much cheaper and always much richer in Vitamin C. Furthermore, it is delicious, and there is quite a large range of flavours among the different types of cabbage. Very young Brussels sprouts make an excellent salad treated the same way.

Ingredients (to serve 4–5)

1 small firm white cabbage
1 small onion
1 or 2 CLOVES OF GARLIC (optional, but either leave it out or use it fairly lavishly)

½ teacup MAYONNAISE
½ teacup vinegar
2 lumps sugar
2 level teasp. mustard or CARAWAY SEEDS

Utensils

Sharp knife
Colander
Small saucepan

Clean cloth
Salad bowl

Time required: 10–15 mins.

Method

1. Slice cabbage into quarters. Wash well in cold salted water. Cut out stalk and shred rest finely. Place in colander and wash again under running cold water. Shake and gently dab dry.
2. Peel onion and chop fairly coarsely. Peel and chop garlic finely.
3. Put cabbage, onion, and garlic in salad bowl, with a little salt and pepper. Add mayonnaise and mustard or CARAWAY SEEDS.
4. Boil sugar with vinegar and pour over salad. Mix

thoroughly, using your hands. Allow to stand about 15 mins. before serving.

A cabbage salad may also be made with a simple FRENCH DRESSING and a handful of raisins in place of the seeds.

Apple Salad

Apples and cheese go together like bacon and eggs. This makes a good light lunch, with wholemeal bread and two or three cheeses to choose from. It can also accompany cold meats – particularly pork.

Ingredients (to serve 4)

2 eating apples, as sharp-
  flavoured as possible
1 head of celery
1 rounded tablesp. shelled
  walnuts
1 rounded tablesp. raisins

Dressing
3 tablesp. cream or top of milk
1 tablesp. leamon juice
Pinch sugar
Pepper and salt

Utensils

Knife and chopping board
Strainer

Clean cloth

Time required: 10–15 mins.

Method

1. Peel apples, cut into quarters, remove core, and chop roughly.
2. Wash and dry celery and cut all the white part into small pieces. Don't forget the thick stump at the bottom – trim it clean and DICE it; it has a delicious nutty flavour. Keep the outside of the celery for soups or stews.
3. Put nuts in strainer, rinse, dry, and chop roughly. Put raisins in strainer, rinse under running water, dry well.
4. Mix all ingredients together and dress, adding salt and pepper to taste.

To make a more substantial salad, add shredded white cabbage, as much or as little as you like.

Cucumber Salad with Yoghourt

A cucumber salad is always good with a French dressing and a little chopped onion and parsley, but served with YOGHOURT it makes an interesting hors d'œuvre. You can also eat it with cold meats or fish.

Ingredients (to serve 4 or 5)

1 cucumber (ridge or long green will do equally well)	4 tablesp. WINE VINEGAR
	Salt
1 small jar of natural YOGHOURT	CAYENNE PEPPER

Utensils

Knife	Clean cloth
Strainer	

Time required: 5–10 mins. plus at least 1 hr to stand.

Method

1. Peel cucumber and slice thinly, laying slices in shallow dish. Sprinkle not too thickly with salt. Leave to stand for an hour or so. (The salt draws the liquid from the cucumber and makes it more digestible.)

2. Pour off liquid, put cucumber in strainer, and rinse well under cold tap. Pat dry.

3. Arrange slices attractively in shallow dish, sprinkle with vinegar and pour YOGHOURT over, leaving a border of cucumber uncovered if possible. Sprinkle YOGHOURT with CAYENNE PEPPER.

Vegetable Dishes

Apart from the fact that they are delicious, we cannot do without vegetables, salads, and fruits, which together give us almost all the Vitamin C we get and which we *must* have if we are to be healthy. So eat all you can of all three of them. Here are a few ways in which to enjoy vegetables.

Cauliflower Cheese (au gratin)

This is an excellent light lunch or supper dish. If you add hard-boiled eggs, the meal will be more substantial, but they are not essential.

Ingredients (to serve 4)

1 fairly large cauliflower	¾ pt thick cheese sauce (see
4 eggs (optional)	p. 107)
Salt	A tablesp. fresh or dried
A NUT of butter	BREADCRUMBS

Utensils

1 small saucepan (for eggs)	Ovenware dish
1 medium saucepan, with well-fitting lid	Colander
	Basin
Chopping knife and board, or parsley-mincer	Utensils for making cheese sauce

Time required: About ½ hr

Method

1. Wash cauliflower thoroughly, cut into large sprigs, chop a few of the best green leaves.

2. Heat about 1 in. water in pan, add level teasp. salt, and, when boiling, put in sprigs, cover with lid, and boil steadily for 10–15 mins. – not too rapidly, or water will boil away.

3. Meanwhile, make cheese sauce (p. 107), keeping back about 1 dessertsp. cheese.

4. Chop parsley, about 1 teasp. Boil eggs hard (if using).

5. Peel eggs (if using) and cut in two lengthwise.

6. Drain cauliflower (keeping water for STOCK).

7. Arrange sprigs in ovenware dish with halved eggs round edges (if using). Pour sauce over. Sprinkle with remaining cheese and BREADCRUMBS. DOT with butter.

8. Place dish under hot grill for a few moments, to brown top.

9. Sprinkle with parsley and serve.

NOTE: Some of the water from vegetables boiled this way may be kept for making gravies or adding to stock. It contains valuable mineral salts and vitamins.

Cauliflower Sprigs

When you cook cauliflower as an accompaniment to meat, it is not necessary to keep it whole. If you break it into small sprigs, you can cook it in less water and more quickly, thus retaining the precious vitamins instead of boiling them all away. Cook the sprigs in a very little boiling salted water, in a covered saucepan, for 3 or 4 mins. only. They should then be tender but still crisp. Drain well, and toss them in a little butter melted in the same saucepan over a low flame for 1 min. Sprinkle with chopped parsley, salt, and pepper – and you won't need any of that billposter's paste often described as 'white sauce'.

Chicory with Ham and Cheese Sauce

Chicory, imported from Belgium together with various methods of cooking it, is regularly seen in our shops now when in season. You can braise it, eat it raw in salads, or cook it as follows. It has a faintly bitter taste which many people find piquant and a few dislike. You may, if you like, eliminate this by BLANCHING for 5 mins. before further cooking. See under Chicory, p. 195.

Ingredients (to serve 4)

4 heads of chicory (short fat ones all about the same size)	4 large slices of cooked ham 1 pt cheese sauce (see p. 107)

Utensils

1 ovenware casserole (it can be shallow but must have a wide base) Knife	Spoon Clean cloth Greaseproof paper Utensils for cheese sauce

Time required: From $1\frac{1}{4}$–$1\frac{3}{4}$ hrs

Method

1. Set oven to Warm, Mark 3, 335°F. Put casserole in oven to warm.
2. Wash chicory; trim off a thin slice from the bottom and discard any discoloured leaves. Dry.
3. Wrap each head of chicory in a slice of ham and lay them side by side in the casserole.
4. Make 1 pt cheese sauce and pour it over the chicory.
5. Place piece of greaseproof paper on top. Cover casserole with lid, and cook in centre of oven until chicory is tender – for 1–$1\frac{1}{2}$ hrs, according to size of pieces. Reduce heat to Mark 2, 310°F., at about half-time.

Serve in casserole.

Stuffed Tomatoes

These are excellent by themselves as a light meal, or they can be served as an accompaniment to various meat dishes. You may vary the stuffing, using anchovies or cheese instead of meat. Stuffed with cheese, they go particularly well with veal.

Ingredients (to serve 6)

6 large tomatoes
1 tablesp. olive oil (or dripping)
1 small onion or shallot
1 very small CLOVE of GARLIC (optional)
1 rasher streaky bacon
$\frac{1}{2}$ cup fresh breadcrumbs

1 slice ham (or a little minced, left-over cold meat or 2 oz. fresh, finely-minced beef or veal)
$\frac{1}{2}$ oz. butter
Parsley
Salt
Pepper

Utensils

Ovenware dish
Frying-pan

Knife
Parsley-mincer (if available)

Chopping knife and board
Scissors
Basin
Wooden spoon

Teaspoon
Sieve or strainer
Cloth

Time required: About $\frac{3}{4}$ hr

Method

1. Set oven to Mark 4, Moderate, 355° F.
2. Wash and dry tomatoes and cut a slice from the top of each.
3. Scoop out pulp from this slice and about half the pulp from the tomato. Rub this through sieve into basin, with wooden spoon.
4. Peel and chop onion finely; also GARLIC if using. Chop ham very small. Cut bacon into very small pieces with scissors. Mince parsley – about 2 teasp.
5. Heat olive oil in pan and gently fry onion, GARLIC, and bacon together for 3 or 4 mins. until soft. Mix this straight from pan with tomato pulp.
6. Make fresh BREADCRUMBS. Add to rest, together with chopped ham, parsley, a little salt and pepper.
7. Stuff the tomatoes with this mixture. Sprinkle a few BREADCRUMBS on top, and put a tiny piece of butter on each.
8. Arrange in ovenware dish and bake for about 20 mins.

Serve in dish, garnished with parsley.

Mushrooms fried with Onion

Mushrooms are delicious alone and go well with almost any other food. They are wonderful with a dish of crisp bacon. For the following way of cooking them you need the large, dark ones. Real field mushrooms, freshly picked, are, of course, the ideal.

Ingredients (to serve 4)

¾ lb. large mushrooms	3–4 tablesp. salad oil
1 large onion	Salt
1 CLOVE of GARLIC	Pepper
(optional)	Parsley

Utensils

Medium or large frying-pan	Chopping knife and board
FISH SLICE	Clean cloth
Knife	

Time required: About 20 mins.

Method

1. Wash the mushrooms, but do not peel (most of the flavour is in the skin). Cut off most of stalk and put aside for stews or soup. Dab dry gently.
2. Peel and chop onion and garlic fairly fine.
3. Heat salad oil in pan – beware of having it too hot. Put in mushrooms, stalk side uppermost, and fry gently for 10 mins.
4. Chop parsley.
5. Turn mushrooms, add onion and garlic, and fry another five mins. or a little more.
6. Serve on hot dish, sprinkled with salt, pepper, and parsley.

Besides bringing out the best in bacon, these are excellent with steaks, chops, sausages, and some fish dishes.

Spring Carrots

Young carrots, especially when freshly pulled from the garden, are almost a different vegetable from the mature ones we eat in our stews in the winter, and are delicious with almost any meat dish. The simplest way to cook and serve them is, I think, the best. Buy them in bunches with their leaves.

Ingredients (to serve 4)

About 1¼ lb. of carrots (after removal of the green tops). The smaller the carrots the better

1 oz. butter

1 teasp. sugar

Salt and pepper

Parsley and (if you can get it) a little CHERVIL

Utensils

1 medium saucepan

Knife

Parsley-mincer, or chopping knife and board

Colander

Basin

Time required: ¼ hr to prepare, 10 mins, or a little more to cook.

Method

1. Scrub and trim carrots. Leave very small ones whole, but if they are larger cut them in thick slices. To look nice, they should be all whole or all sliced.
2. Put sufficient water in pan to cover carrots, bring to the boil with 1 teasp. salt, add sugar, put in carrots, and cook fairly fast until tender – 10–15 mins.
3. Chop parsley and CHERVIL if using.
4. Drain in colander over basin. (Keep water for STOCK.)
5. Melt butter in pan, toss carrots for a minute or two until all are well buttered, sprinkle with parsley (and CHERVIL).
6. Serve in heated dish.

Lettuce as a cooked vegetable

Lettuces are the one vegetable grown by everyone with a patch of garden, and invariably they come along in a great glut just when they are cheapest in the shops, and the embarrassed gardener can't give them away. If you get tired of them as salad, try cooking them. They make a pleasant change.

Ingredients (to serve 4)

2 hearty lettuces (preferably   1 oz. butter or margarine
    cos)   Salt

Utensils

1 medium saucepan, with lid   Spoon

Time required: 5–10 mins.

Method

1. Cut the lettuces lengthwise into four or five pieces, wash thoroughly, and shake off as much surplus water as you can.

2. Melt butter in pan, put in lettuces as closely packed as possible, sprinkle with salt and pepper, cover, and cook on rather low heat, turning once or twice with spoon so that all the lettuce gets equally cooked. Young ones will be cooked in about 5 mins., older ones will take longer. It does not matter if the thick part of the heart is still a little crisp, but do not overcook.

If you serve a dish of green peas, well buttered, at the same time, and some wholemeal bread and butter, you have an excellent light meal.

Green Beans with Butter
(Haricots verts au beurre)

A large helping of tender young runner beans, or French beans, with nothing else but butter, makes a lunch or supper dish second to none. If it is not sufficiently substantial for you, cheese and wholemeal bread will fill the gap.

Ingredients (for a main dish)

½–¾ lb. runner beans per person

1½–2 oz. butter per person
Salt and pepper

Utensils

1 large and 1 medium saucepan
Sharp knife
Large spoon

Bean-slicer (if you have one and want to save time)
Colander
Basin

Time required: To prepare: this depends entirely on your skill and the amount of beans. To cook: about 10 mins.

Method

1. Wash the beans, 'top-and-tail' them, and remove any strings along the edges with a knife (if they are young, there should be very few).
2. If young, snap beans into two or three pieces; if older, slice diagonally with knife, not too fine, or use slicer. (Most bean-slicers cut the beans too fine, and much of the flavour and the food value is lost in the cooking.)
3. Have ready large saucepan with sufficient boiling water to cover beans, and about 1 small teasp. salt to every pound of beans.
4. Put in beans, bring to the boil, and skim off scum which rises. Cook without lid for shortest possible time, skimming off scum once or twice; begin to test by biting one or two beans after 5 mins., as young beans will cook very quickly. The finer they are cut, the quicker they will cook. If you cook them too long, they will lose their fresh green colour and much of their flavour and value.
5. As soon as soft, strain into colander over basin (keeping some of the water for STOCK if you like).
6. The saucepan will have a tide-line of scum, so melt butter in clean pan, and toss the beans in it for a few moments with a little pepper until all are well buttered. CORRECT SEASONING.
7. Serve in hot dish.

Jacket Potatoes

Everyone thinks he knows how to boil potatoes, but how many people cook them in their skins, which nine times out of ten is the sensible way? First, the flavour is much better; second, valuable vitamins are preserved; and third, it is no more trouble to peel them after cooking than before (and considerably less if you don't peel them at all). At a time when winter potatoes are very bad and apt to have insect holes or patches of discoloration owing to disease or frost, it is justifiable and necessary to peel them. Otherwise, scrub them well, put them into boiling salted water, and when they are done, peel them by holding the hot potato with a fork or a clean cloth (or wear rubber gloves) and skinning them thinly and cleanly with a small knife. New potatoes should then be tossed in a little butter or margarine and sprinkled with chopped parsley. A knob of butter on old potatoes is an improvement too, and a thick sprinkling of parsley. Parsley should be used really lavishly in the kitchen, not only for its flavour and its decorative qualities, but because it is rich in Vitamin C, and iron, although you need to eat a great deal of it to obtain a significant contribution to your daily intake of the vitamin.

Ingredients

1 sound, very large or medium-large potato per person (according to appetites)

Olive oil (or melted bacon fat)
Salt

Utensils

Fork
Clean cloth
Saucer

Pastry-brush or butter paper
Skewer or pointed knife

Time required: 45 mins.–1¼ hrs

Method

1. Set oven to Hot, Mark 7, 425° F.
2. Scrub each potato very thoroughly. Dry. Prick once or twice on each side with fork.
3. Put a little olive oil in a saucer, and with pastry-brush (or butter paper) coat each potato with film of oil.
4. Sprinkle each potato with salt – not too heavily.
5. Cook on shelf about the middle of the oven until tender. Test by thrusting skewer or pointed knife into largest potato.

Serve heaped in a dish with a sprig or two of parsley or other greenery. They should be split open lengthwise at table, a good knob of butter inserted, and closed again for a minute or two. The skin, cooked this way, will be crisp and nutty and can be eaten with the rest.

Excellent with cold meat and a salad.

Stuffed Jacket Potatoes

This makes a light meal by itself.

First cook the potatoes exactly as above. The stuffing is as follows:

Ingredients

1 egg per potato   Salt and pepper
A little butter

Utensils

Ovenware dish   Teaspoon
Sharp knife

Time required: About $\frac{1}{4}$ hr after potatoes are cooked.

Method

1. Take cooked potatoes from oven, but do not turn off heat.

2. Slice the tops from the potatoes $\frac{1}{2}$–1 in. thick.

3. Scoop out with the teaspoon sufficient from each potato to leave room for an egg to be broken into the hole. Make sure the holes are deep enough. The egg should lie just below the surface of the potato.

4. Break an egg into each potato, add a little salt and pepper and a knob of butter.

5. Replace tops on potatoes, stand them upright in ovenware dish, and return to oven for 5 mins.

Serve garnished with sprigs of parsley or a celery leaf.

Keep the potato scooped from the holes for frying up with the breakfast bacon. You can stuff potatoes with other things besides eggs; grated cheese, for instance, or fried bacon and mushrooms chopped small.

Chip Potatoes

Well-made chips should be crisp and crunchy on the outside and soft inside. To obtain this result, they should be cooked in oil.

Ingredients

$\frac{1}{2}$ lb. potatoes per person (or more), large, long ones if possible

Plenty of any good cooking oil, 1 pt minimum

Salt

Utensils

Chip-pan with basket or deep, thick saucepan and FISH SLICE

Potato-peeler or knife

Potato-chipper, if available

Colander

Clean cloth

Absorbent paper

Large basin

Time required: About 10 mins. to cook, plus preparation time according to quantity.

Method

1. Peel the potatoes. Cut them in halves lengthwise, then again lengthwise, and then into the size you require. Or use a potato-chipper. Put them into a basin of cold water as you do them.

2. Have the pan not more than half full of oil: it is dangerous to fill it more. Heat gently until the oil is very hot – that is after it has ceased to bubble and a faint blue haze is rising. A way to test the heat is to drop a cube of stale bread into the oil; if it goes pale gold the oil is too cold, if it goes dark brown the oil is too hot – it should go golden brown almost at once if the oil is at the correct temperature.

3. Drain the chips and dry well. If they are wet, the fat will spit dangerously. Have a dish heating in the oven and absorbent paper handy.

4. Put chips into basket and lower basket gently into hot fat. Or put as many as you can manage at a time into the oil with the fish-slice. Don't *drop* them in, unless you want painful burns. Do not fry too many at a time, or the temperature of the fat will be lowered and the chips soggy. Cook them until they are soft and a pale gold colour. Then take them out with basket or FISH-SLICE and put on to absorbent paper in hot dish in oven until all are done.

5. Reheat the oil and put all chips back together, being careful not to splash, for 1 min. only. They will at once crisp and turn gold. Remove from oil on to a fresh piece of paper, placed in the hot dish, sprinkle with salt, and serve at once, pulling the paper out from under the chips before putting the dish on the table.

If you do not require the chips immediately but have to prepare meat or fish first, you can keep them warm for as long as you like before doing the final cooking – but be sure to get the oil really hot again.

T–D

Sauté Potatoes

This is an excellent way to serve potatoes with grills or chops or fish, bacon and eggs – almost anything. You can use up left-overs, or prepare mountains of potatoes in advance and sauté them in a few minutes.

Simply boil the potatoes first (smallish waxy ones are best for this), preferably in their skins which you remove as soon as the potatoes are cool enough to handle easily. When half or quite cold, slice them or cut into small pieces. Then fry them quickly in a very little shallow fat, which must be very hot, tossing them so that all sides are browned.

Potatoes Lyonnaises

Done the same way, but a little chopped onion is first half fried in the fat, then the potatoes are put in and they are finished together. Serve sprinkled with chopped parsley, salt, and pepper.

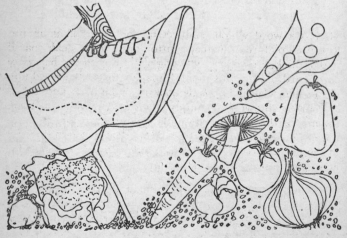

Meat Dishes

Stew is a word which conjures up for many of us an unfortunate picture of watery mutton or cubes of steak coated with a thick, brown gravy tasting of nothing so much as salty cardboard. Forget this mental image – forget the word too, if you like. Call it *ragoût* or cook it in the oven and call it *en casserole*. Stewing is simply a method of slow cooking, usually of the cheaper though equally nourishing cuts of meat. There are innumerable different variations of the stew in the cooking of every country, and I do not apologize for giving you several to introduce my recipes for cooking meat.

NOTE: There are excellent heavy enamelled pans in splendid colours on the market suitable both for stewing on top of the cooker or as casseroles in the oven, and handsome enough to bring to table.

Les Carbonnades Flamandes
(Beef stewed in Beer)

The Belgians stew beef in beer. It makes a rich and appetizing dish, but the flavour of beer is not strong enough to discourage the younger members of the family.

Ingredients (to serve 4)

1¼–1½ lb. chuck steak or other stewing steak

1½–2 oz. dripping (or other cooking fat)

About ¾ lb. onions

½ pt beer – brown ale is best, but any beer will serve

2 level dessertsp. sugar – preferably brown

BOUQUET GARNI

2 or 3 tablesp. SEASONED FLOUR

Pepper and salt

A crust of bread

French mustard

Utensils

Knife

Perforated spoon

Dessert spoon

Large plate

Frying-pan

Ovenware casserole with lid

Time required: About 2½ hrs

Method

1. Set oven to Slow, Mark 2, 310° F. Put casserole in to warm.
2. Peel and slice onions fairly thickly.
3. Cut meat into slices about ½ in. thick and 2 or 3 in. square (size is unimportant).
4. Put seasoned flour on plate and roll pieces of meat in it until they are well coated.
5. Melt most of the dripping in frying-pan, put in onions, and fry gently for about 10 mins., turning often.
6. Take onions from pan with perforated spoon and put into warmed casserole.

7. Now turn up heat under frying-pan and into the same dripping put as many pieces of meat as there is room for without overlapping. The heat must be strong but not fierce; the object is to seal the juices into the meat by browning the outside quickly. Brown first one side then the other – about 1 min. each side should be sufficient. As each is done, add it to the onions in the casserole and make room for another piece. Add a little more dripping if it seems necessary.

8. When all meat is browned and in the casserole, turn down the heat under the frying-pan and pour the beer into the pan. Stir it round to take up any juices left from the meat and onions, and pour this brew into the casserole. Add the sugar, a little salt and pepper, and the BOUQUET GARNI. The meat should *just* be covered. If it is not add a little water.

9. Put a thick layer of French mustard on the crumb side of the crust of bread, and place it mustard side down on top of the rest. Cover with lid.

10. Cook in middle of oven for at least 2 hrs. Serve in the casserole, but remove the crust.

Serve with plain boiled potatoes sprinkled with plenty of parsley.

If it is more convenient, this or any other stew can equally well be cooked on a very low heat on top of the cooker, if necessary with an ASBESTOS MAT, provided the saucepan has a well-fitting lid.

MORE ADVANCED

Bœuf à la Camarguaise
(Beef stewed with Orange Peel, Mushrooms, and Olives)

Yet another stew, cooked in the way they do it in the Camargue district of France. This is a more extravagant dish, excellent for a special party of about eight persons or more – because there is nothing to do at the last minute but simply take it from the oven. During the last half-hour of the cooking, cook plain boiled rice to go with it (see p. 104).

Ingredients (to serve 7 or 8)

2 lb. chuck steak (or other stewing steak)
4 oz. streaky bacon
6 large onions
½ lb. mushrooms
1 small tin tomato purée
2 tablesp. olive oil
1 or 2 thin strips of orange peel

Salt
Pepper
2 tablesp. SEASONED FLOUR
BOUQUET GARNI
6 cloves
1 or 2 CLOVES OF GARLIC
3 or 4 medium-size potatoes (waxy type, if possible)
¼ lb. olives, black if possible

Utensils

Meat knife
Scissors
Tin-opener
Tablespoon
Perforated spoon

Potato-peeler or sharp knife
Frying-pan
Ovenware casserole with lid
Plate

Time required: About 3 hrs

Method

1. Peel and slice onions. Peel and cut garlic into 3 or 4 pieces. Cut bacon into pieces about 1 in. square with scissors. Wash orange, and take off (preferably with potato-peeler) 1 or 2 very thin strips of orange peel, avoiding pith.

2. Set oven to Slow, Mark 2, 310° F. Put casserole in to warm.

3. Heat oil in frying-pan and very gently fry onions and bacon together until onions are golden coloured – about 10 mins.

4. Remove casserole from oven. Lift onions from pan with perforated spoon and place in warmed casserole.

5. Turn up heat under pan. Add a little more olive oil if

necessary. Fry pieces of meat, first on one side then on the other, about 1 min. each side, to seal in the juices. Do only as many as will go comfortably in the pan together, putting them in the casserole as they are done to make way for more.

6. When all meat is browned and in the casserole, add warm water, but do not cover the meat – the water should be about ½ in. below. Add garlic, pepper, very little salt (remember the bacon is salty), the BOUQUET GARNI, cloves, and orange peel. Cover and cook in centre of oven for about 1¾ hrs.

7. After meat has cooked this length of time, peel potatoes and cut into dice about ¾ in. square. Wash mushrooms well and cut into fairly small pieces, including stalks. Open tin of tomato PURÉE.

8. Remove casserole from oven and add all these ingredients, stir well, replace lid, and return to oven for another ¾ hr at least.

9. Just before serving, stir in olives.

Serve with plain boiled rice. Runner beans would go well with this dish, if you wish to serve another vegetable, or grill some tomatoes sprinkled with chopped garlic, salt, and pepper, turn the casserole into a large heated dish, and garnish it with the tomatoes.

Stewed Beef with Sweet- and Sour-Beans

This is a Jewish recipe. It is absolutely splendid when there is a glut of runner beans either in your garden or in the shops. It is very easy to do and quite an inexpensive meal.

Ingredients (to serve 4)

1–1¼ lb. chuck steak or other stewing beef	1 bay leaf
	Salt and pepper

1½ lb. runner beans
3 medium-size onions
½ pt STOCK, or water and a
    beef extract cube

3 level tablesp. flour
3 level tablesp. brown sugar
3 tablesp. vinegar

Utensils

2 medium saucepans, one
    with well-fitting lid
Meat knife
Bean-slicer or small sharp
    knife
Spoon

Ladle
Basin
Fork or skewer
Colander
Clean cloth

Time required: About 2¼ hrs

Method

1. Wipe meat with damp cloth. Cut it into slices about ½ in.
   thick and 2 or 3 in. 'square'. The size is unimportant.
2. Put meat in pan with well-fitting lid, with stock (or
   water and cube), pepper, salt, bay leaf, and bring
   slowly to SIMMERING point.
3. Peel and slice onions fairly thinly, and add to meat.
   Cover pan and simmer slowly for about 2 hrs, or until
   meat is tender when tested with fork or skewer.
4. Meanwhile, wash beans, string and slice them (not too
   finely).
5. When meat has cooked about 1½ hrs, fill second saucepan
   with water, add 1 teasp. salt, bring water to boil, and put
   in beans. Cook 10–15 mins., or until tender. Drain.
6. While beans are cooking, mix flour and sugar in basin
   with a little pepper and salt. Mix to a thin paste with
   vinegar.
7. Now ladle some of the liquor out of the meat saucepan
   and pour it slowly on the flour and sugar, stirring briskly
   with the other hand. Add a second ladleful and stir well.
8. Turn this mixture back into the meat saucepan. Stir all
   well, cover and cook gently another 10 or 15 mins.
9. Taste the liquor in the saucepan. It should be quite
   sweet and also quite sour. If you think it could do with

either more sugar or more vinegar, add them at this
point. It is very much a matter of taste.

10. Add the cooked beans to the rest. Stir well. Allow
another 5 mins. for the beans to heat through, and serve
on a meat dish or in an attractive casserole.

Serve with plain boiled potatoes.

MORE ADVANCED

Blanquette of Veal
(with Rice)

This simply means a 'white' stew of veal. The best veal is
very expensive nowadays, but a cheap cut is perfectly satisfactory for a *blanquette*.

When BUYING VEAL, ask the butcher if it has been bred
by the currently popular and extremely cruel factory farming
method. If the butcher is honest, the answer, unfortunately,
is more likely than not to be in the affirmative. In that case, I
would suggest that you refuse the meat and choose something
else, making your reasons clear. In any case, meat bred by
these methods is hardly worth eating, but unless we all make
a great fuss about it, I am afraid that, before long, there
won't be any other kind.

As indicated, this recipe is rather more complicated than
others in this book but the result is fairly impressive. Study
it well before starting, and give yourself plenty of time. There
are several operations, none of them difficult, but they must
be co-ordinated. Be sure to serve both *blanquette* and rice in
hot dishes.

Ingredients (to serve 4)

1½ lb. stewing veal (breast or shoulder or thick end of the neck)	1 lemon
	1¼ oz. flour
	About 3 oz. butter
1 onion, 1 CLOVE, 1 carrot	Nutmeg and parsley

1 stalk of celery (if available)
Salt, pepper, and peppercorns
BOUQUET GARNI
2–3 oz. mushrooms
About 8 tiny onions or
 SHALLOTS – or cut up a
 large onion

1 yolk of egg
About 2 tablesp. cream or top
 of milk
8 rounded tablesp. Patna
 rice

Utensils

1 large saucepan
1 medium saucepan with
 well-fitting lid
2 small saucepans
Sharp knife
Lemon-squeezer
Grater
2 cups
Wooden spoon

Parsley-mincer, or chopping
 knife and board
Spoon
Skewer
Measuring jug
Plate
Straining-spoon
Clean cloth
Kettle
Strainer

Time required: About 2 hrs

Method

1. Wipe meat with clean, damp cloth. Cut into pieces
 about 1½–2 in. square, removing any tough skin. Don't
 worry about the papery tissues that seem to be every-
 where – they disappear in the cooking.
2. Put pieces of meat in the medium pan and cover with
 a little over 1½ pts of cold water. Add a small teasp. salt.
 Bring it slowly to the boil, taking about half an hour
 over it, and skimming off the scum as it rises. Stir
 occasionally to bring all scum to the top. (This is known
 as BLANCHING.)
3. Meanwhile, peel the onion and stick the CLOVE in it.
 Wash celery, scrub or scrape carrot. When the BLANCH-
 ING is finished, add these vegetables to the veal together
 with 6 peppercorns and the BOUQUET GARNI, cover
 pan, turn down heat, and cook gently for 1–1¼ hrs, or
 until meat is tender when tested with skewer.

4. While this is going on peel the little onions or SHALLOTS; wash but do not peel mushrooms and cut them into four or more pieces according to size.

5. Melt 1 oz. butter in small pan, put in onions and about 2 tablesp. water, and cook very gently for about 10 mins.

6. Squeeze the lemon and add the juice to the onions. Add mushrooms and a little salt and pepper. Continue to cook very gently for another 10–20 mins., stirring from time to time. Watch that they do not go dry (add a little more water if there seems any danger). When onions are soft but not pappy, remove from heat.

7. Boil 4 pts water in a large pan with a heaped teasp. salt.

8. Wash rice in strainer. When water in pan is boiling, put the rice in and boil fast for 15 mins. approximately. Since rice varies, test to see if cooked by pressing or biting a few grains; if not quite cooked, continue boiling till soft. In the meantime put a kettle of water on to boil for separating the rice.

9. When the veal is cooked, lift meat from pan with straining spoon, leaving liquor. Set meat aside on plate. Cover with lid to keep warm.

10. Melt 1½ oz. of butter in small pan, stir in just over 1 oz. of flour. Cook for one or two minutes, stirring with wooden spoon. This is called a ROUX.

11. Pour liquor from veal into ROUX, stirring vigorously over medium heat until you have a thin, creamy sauce. Turn back into larger saucepan and add the onions and mushrooms in the liquor in which they were cooked. Grate a little nutmeg into this. Cook gently together for about 10 mins.

12. When rice is cooked, turn into strainer. Have kettle of water boiling, hold strainer over sink and pour boiling water steadily over rice to separate grains. Turn rice into hot dish, add knob of butter, and keep hot in oven.

13. Break eggs, SEPARATING WHITE FROM YOLK in two cups. Cover white and put aside. (It will keep in refrigerator or cool place until required for glazing pastry, making meringues, etc.) Add cream or top of milk to yolk.

14. Remove pan with onions, etc., from heat, spoon some of the liquor into cup of egg and cream, mix well, return to pan, stirring steadily. Add cooked meat to this sauce, stir all well, return to low heat for a minute or two, stirring constantly. *Do not allow to boil.*

15. CORRECT SEASONING. Chop parsley, and sprinkle over just before serving in heated dish.

Pot-Roasted Veal
(with Onions and Cheese)

See note on buying veal in previous recipe

Cheese goes with veal almost as well as apples go with cheese – they just seem to have a natural affinity. This is a good dish to do for a dinner for any number. Any size of joint can be cooked this way, provided you have a good, solid saucepan or fireproof casserole large enough to take it. It need not be an expensive cut, either. You may also do a pot-roast on top of the stove on a low heat instead of in the oven.

Ingredients

Piece of veal, any cut, weighing about 2 lb. without bone
3 oz. butter
1 or 2 sprigs or 1 teasp. powdered rosemary
1½ lb. onions
¼ pt good STOCK (meat extract or gravy cube made up with rather less water than usual will do)
Salt and pepper
3 oz. cheese (Parmesan or a strong Cheddar)

Utensils

A strong casserole of the type that goes on an open flame, or saucepan with well-fitting lid
1 medium saucepan
Knife
Grater
Tablespoon
Large plate
Clean cloth

Time required: 1¾ hrs

Method

1. Turn oven to Moderate, Mark 4, 355° F.
2. Wipe meat with damp cloth. Sprinkle it with SEASON-ED FLOUR, either from a DREDGER, or by putting flour on plate and rolling meat in it. Shake off surplus.
3. Heat 1 tablesp. butter in casserole or saucepan. When it ceases to froth, put in meat and brown it, turning from side to side, leaving each side a minute or two, until all sides are lightly browned.
4. Sprinkle rosemary over meat, put on lid, and cook very gently for 1½ hrs on middle shelf in oven.
5. Meanwhile, peel and slice onions fairly thinly.
6. Melt rest of butter except 1 teasp. in second saucepan, and cook onions very gently, stirring often. They must MELT rather than fry, and be quite soft and a pale gold colour when done. Remove from heat.
7. Grate cheese.
8. When meat is cooked, remove lid from casserole, pour in stock, stir, and BASTE meat well.
9. Sprinkle grated cheese over meat, DOT with rest of butter, turn up heat to Very Hot, and close oven again for a few minutes, until cheese is lightly browned.
10. Reheat onions and turn on to heated meat dish. Serve joint on bed of onions, surrounded by gravy from casserole.

The joint should be carved at table, and cheese and onions shared carefully among the diners. Roast or mashed potatoes and almost any vegetable may accompany it, but braised chicory is superb.

Wiener Schnitzel

See note on buying veal on p. 83

This is a favourite Austrian way of frying a thin slice of veal. The name means literally 'Viennese Slice'. It is very simple to do, but must be done with good-quality meat.

Ingredients (to serve 4)

4 thin slices of ESCALOPES
from the leg or fillet of
veal, about 1–1½ lb.
Half a lemon
Flour
1 egg (part of another may
be necessary)
Salt and pepper

Fine FRESH BREADCRUMBS,
about 5 heaped tablesp.
Butter for frying, about 3 oz.
Optional: 8 fillets of anchovy
(you can buy these by
weight at delicatessen
shops, or in tins at any
grocer's)

Utensils

Rolling-pin, for beating
meat
Large frying-pan
Sharp knife
FISH-SLICE

Grater for crumbs
1 soup-plate or shallow dish
2 sheets paper, or flat dishes
1 dish large enough to hold
all 4 schnitzels

Time required: About ¾ hr

Method

1. Lay each slice of veal in turn on a wooden board or clean
   table and beat it with a rolling-pin until it is flattened
   out to less than ¼ in. thick and takes up a lot more room
   than before. (Some butchers will do this for you.)
2. Nick the edges with a sharp knife, to prevent the slices
   from curling up.
3. Make BREADCRUMBS
4. Beat egg with a little salt and pepper in soup-plate. One
   egg may not be quite enough for 4 schnitzels; if you have
   insufficient left when you come to the last one, beat up
   another egg, but pour half into a cup and keep for some
   other use.
5. Put about 2 tablesp. SEASONED FLOUR on one sheet of
   paper, and BREADCRUMBS on the other.
6. Dip each schnitzel first in flour, then in egg, then in
   crumbs, and see that they are well coated each time, but
   shake off surplus. Leave for about 10 mins. lying in
   crumbs, to 'set'.

7. Melt butter, and as soon as it has ceased to froth, fry two schnitzels at a time, if your pan is large enough, turning them with fish-slice. About 2 mins. each side should be enough; but if you are not sure they are done, give them a little longer. Add more butter, and fry the next two. Keep heat moderate.

8. You can GARNISH each schnitzel with one or two anchovy fillets if available and a thin slice or two of lemon. More lemon may be handed at table to squeeze on the meat. Decorate with sprigs of parsley.

Serve with creamy mashed potatoes or new potatoes and a lettuce salad – or fresh green peas, young carrots or spinach. These should be prepared before you start on the meat and put on to cook while the schnitzels are 'setting'.

MORE ADVANCED

Mixed Grill with Chips

A mixed grill is more often eaten in a restaurant than at home, though there is no reason in the world why this should be so. Nicely arranged, it is one of the most appetizing-looking meals you can bring to table. You can choose from chops or cutlets, bacon rashers, kidneys, liver, sausages, tomatoes, mushrooms. It is unwise for an inexperienced cook to try to do too complicated a mixture, because the different foods cook at different speeds and you are going to get yourself tied into knots. Unless you have a particularly large grill, don't try to do a mixed grill for more than two or three persons, either – although you can always cheat slightly by

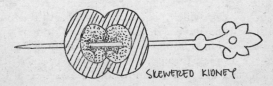

SKEWERED KIDNEY

cooking the sausages and perhaps the mushrooms in a frying-pan at the same time. Steaks should not be included, but should always be cooked as a separate dish with the care and respect they deserve.

Ingredients (to serve 2)

2 mutton chops (loin), or 4 lamb cutlets
4 rashers of bacon, any cut
2 (or 4) sheep's kidneys
2 large sausages or 6 chipolata sausages
2 large or 4 small tomatoes

Small CLOVE OF GARLIC (optional)
2 oz. watercress
A little dripping or salad oil
Potatoes for chips (see p. 74)
Oil for frying chips

Utensils

Fork, spoon
Sharp pointed knife
2 skewers or wooden picks
Chip-pan with basket, or thick saucepan

Small pan or dish for melting dripping
Pastry-brush or butter paper
Clean cloth

Time required: About ¾ hr or less

Method

1. First prepare chips, as explained on p. 74. Cook them and keep warm in colander or chip basket, ready for final crisping. Wash watercress, and shake dry.

2. Turn on grill fully. Put a little dripping in pan under or over grill to melt. Grease grid.

3. Wipe all meat with damp cloth. Prick sausages once or twice. Split kidneys lengthwise, but not right through; remove skin, which comes off easily, and cut out core with pointed knife. (If you break the kidneys apart in doing so, don't despair – they'll taste the same.) Put a skewer or pick through each kidney, to keep it open. Trim rind and RUST from bacon.

4. Arrange chops and sausages in centre of grid. Sprinkle with salt and pepper and brush all over with melted dripping or salad oil.

5. Wash and dry tomatoes and cut in halves (across). Sprinkle with salt and pepper. If using garlic, peel and chop this finely and sprinkle a little on each half tomato. Wash and dry mushrooms. Remove stalks and put aside for stews or stock. If the caps are thick, slice them through once. Arrange tomatoes, mushrooms, and kidneys round the chops and sausages on the outside of the grid where the heat will be less fierce. Brush or dab everything with dripping. Do not put salt on kidneys until after they are cooked – it tends to toughen them. Lay the bacon rashers across the kidneys.

6. Make sure you have dishes heating ready for the mixed grill and for the chips, and a piece of absorbent paper on which to drain the chips.

7. Now place the grid beneath the red-hot grill and cook at top temperature for 1 min. only. Turn everything except tomatoes, and repeat. Then reduce heat to moderate or slightly higher. Watch carefully to see that everything gets a fair share of the heat and not too much. Do not use a fork to turn the chops, or the juices will run out; use a spoon and the flat of a knife.

The different foods will cook at the following approximate times:

Chops: 10–15 mins. according to thickness (cutlets would take rather less)

Sausages: About the same; or about 6 mins. if they are chipolata

Kidneys: 5–10 mins. – they are cooked when little beads of blood ooze out

Tomatoes: 5–10 mins.

Mushrooms: 5–10 mins.

Bacon: 3–4 mins.

Everything will have to be turned at least once more.

8. The bacon will be cooked first. Remove it to hot dish in oven. If the design of your grid makes this possible, BASTE the meats with the hot fat. Otherwise, dab a little more dripping on when you turn them. Grills are apt to heat very unevenly, except on brand-new cookers, and you will have to watch that things on the outside edge are not getting left out altogether. Remove each piece to the hot dish in the oven as it is cooked.

9. Half-way through the cooking, heat up the oil in the chip pan. Watch to see that it does not overheat.

10. As soon as the grilling is finished, arrange everything attractively on the hot dish. Pour the fat into the dripping bowl or a cup – not over the meat. Finish the chips.

11. Arrange the watercress in two bunches at each end of the dish, and serve.

A little Worcester sauce is good with a mixed grill – but never spoil good food by coating it with any thick commercial sauce out of a bottle which happens to be standing around. This is the best way to ruin your palate.

If you want another vegetable, have peas or green beans or fresh young cabbage or cauliflower – in fact almost anything goes with a mixed grill.

MORE ADVANCED

Sauté Kidneys with Rice

Kidneys are one of the most valuable of meat foods, being a rich source of body-building animal protein as well as of vitamins. It is not everyone who likes their somewhat strong flavour, but if you do like them, you are apt to be an addict. One of the nicest ways I know to enjoy them is SAUTÉ with rice. Lambs' kidneys, being the most delicate in flavour, are usually used for this dish, but any other kind may be used. Make sure you know how to deal with the rice (plain boiled rice, p. 104) before starting on the kidneys.

Ingredients (to serve 3 or 4)

6 lambs' kidneys
A scant 2 oz. butter
1 small onion
2 rashers bacon
Salt
Pepper
1 rounded and ½ level tablesp.
   flour

¾ pt good STOCK, or the
   equivalent in clear chicken
   soup cubes and water
¼ lb. mushrooms
A few CHIVES or a little
   parsley
2 tablesp. Patna rice per
   person

Utensils

Large saucepan for rice
2 medium saucepans
Small saucepan
Perforated spoon
Wooden spoon
Chopping knife and board

Scissors
Sharp knife
Fork
Strainer
Clean cloth

Time required: ½–¾ hr

Method

1. Put water to boil with salt, for rice. Wash rice. As soon as water boils, put rice in. Keep an eye on it while cooking kidneys, and do not overcook.

2. Turn oven to Slow and have large meat dish heating, also extra dish for keeping kidneys hot.

3. Split kidneys, remove skin and core, and cut into slices.

4. Peel and chop onion fairly fine. Remove rind and RUST from bacon and cut into pieces about the size of a stamp. Wash mushrooms, dab dry, put stalks aside for use in STOCKS or stews, and slice caps into 2 or 3 pieces. Wash and chop CHIVES or parsley.

5 Melt half the butter in a saucepan, put in bacon, and fry gently for 1 min. Add onion and cook gently 3 or 4 mins. until soft, stirring occasionally.

6. Now add sliced kidneys, with a little pepper but not salt, and cook gently, turning once, until colour changes.

Then lift everything out of fat with perforated spoon and keep hot on extra dish in oven.

Don't forget the rice. Stir occasionally. Have you got a kettle of water nearly at the boil?

7. Make a ROUX by putting the flour into the hot fat and cooking very gently, stirring with wooden spoon, until it turns light brown – about 2 mins.

8. Meanwhile, warm stock in small pan. If using soup cubes, dissolve them in half the amount of boiling water and make up to full amount with cold, so that the stock is only warm.

9. Remove ROUX from heat and make sauce thus: add a little of the warm stock, stir until smooth, add rest of stock, return to heat, bring to boil stirring constantly, and cook gently for 5 mins.

10. Meanwhile, melt rest of butter in other pan, put in mushrooms, and cook very gently, stirring and turning occasionally, for about 5 mins.

(If you have not already done so, deal with the rice, which must certainly be cooked by now. Drain, and turn on to meat dish, leaving a large hollow or hole in the middle, and keep hot in oven.)

11. After sauce has cooked 5 mins., put in kidneys, onion, bacon, and any liquor, cover pan, and continue to cook another 3 or 4 mins. Add cooked mushrooms, stir all well, and CORRECT SEASONING.

12. Pour the delicious mess into the hollow in the heap of rice – sprinkle with the CHIVES or parsley, and serve.

Halved tomatoes, with salt, pepper, a little chopped garlic (optional), and a dab of butter, grilled for 5 mins., are a good accompaniment to this dish.

Curried Chicken

I hated curry for years, associating it with a greenish-yellow concoction tasting of nothing very much except aged carrots, which we used to get at the school I went to. I cannot claim that the following recipe would be entirely approved of by a connoisseur of curries, who would probably grind his own curry powder from turmeric and other spices; but if you take care to obtain a good-quality prepared curry powder (and there are a number to choose from on the market) and use it fresh, you will have an appetizing curry for which you need not blush if an Indian comes to dinner.

The word 'curry' comes from the Tamil word 'Kari' and means sauce. You can curry almost anything. The recipe is for chicken, but you could equally well use stewing steak or fish. If you enjoy curries, it would be worth your while to obtain a book of curry recipes and learn to grind your own mixture of spices.

Ingredients (to serve 4)

4 joints of frying chicken
About 1 lb. onions or
    SHALLOTS
CLOVE OF GARLIC
2–3 oz. butter
Any fresh vegetables you can
    obtain: 1 or 2 young carrots
    (not old ones – the flavour is
    too strong), a handful of
    beans or peas, 1 or 2 stalks
    of celery, a piece of young
    marrow cut into cubes, a few
    sprigs of cauliflower, half a
    leek, sliced – any or all of
    these, but not too much of
    anything

About 4 level tablesp. curry
    powder, but study
    instructions on the tin, as
    mixtures vary in strength
Salt
1 apple
$\frac{1}{4}$ pt SOUR MILK or STOCK
1 tablesp. sultanas
A few sprigs of mint
    (optional)
Lemon for GARNISH

Utensils

Knife
Frying-pan
Ovenware casserole
Spoon

Cup
Clean cloth
Chopping knife and board

Time required: 3 hrs (or longer)

Method

1. Set oven to Slow, Mark 2, 310° F.
2. Peel and slice onions fairly thickly. Peel and cut garlic into 2 or 3 pieces.
3. Wash and cut up any vegetables to be used.
4. Melt butter in frying-pan, cook onions and garlic very gently, stirring often, for about 10 mins., until pale gold-coloured.
5. Put casserole in oven to warm.
6. Mix curry powder in cup with a very little water, to make a thick paste.
7. Add this to onions and fry gently for another 5 mins., stirring often.
8. Wipe pieces of chicken with damp cloth, add to other ingredients in pan. Fry for a minute or two more, turning pieces once.
9. Peel and core apple and cut into fairly small pieces. Add to pan.
10. Turn all into heated casserole. Add 1 teasp. salt. Add vegetables, SOUR MILK or STOCK, and sultanas.
11. Cover tightly and cook at least 2 hrs in middle of oven. The longer it cooks the better.
12. Just before serving, wash mint and chop finely. Sprinkle over curry.

Serve with plain boiled rice (see p. 104) on a large dish with the rice as a border. Hand mango chutney (or other good chutney) at table. Garnish with half slices of lemon. Other accompaniments to curries are Bombay Duck (which is not duck but dried fish) and Poppadums, a cross between a pancake and a biscuit, both available tinned.

Sausage and Mash

I hope no one will take offence at the suggestion that he or she does not know how to cook this basic English meal; but the Editor tells me that, from her experience, a few hints will not come amiss, so I offer them in general form.

The Sausages

Wipe the sausages with a damp cloth, prick each one once or twice with a fork, then roll them in SEASONED FLOUR. This treatment prevents them from bursting and gives them a nice crusty outside when cooked.

A little good savoury dripping is the best frying medium, though any fat will cook them. It should be fairly hot, but not extremely so, or again they will burst when you put the sausages in the pan; and you need only sufficient to cover the bottom of the pan easily. Move the sausages around with a long-handled spoon or fish slice, and turn them so that they get brown and crisp all over on the outside – then reduce the heat and cook them for at least another ten minutes.

The Mash

If the potatoes are clean and sound, scrub them and cook them in boiling water with a little salt, peeling them when they are cooked. (They take a little longer to cook this way.)

If you must peel them first, do it as thinly as possible; a potato-peeler is more efficient than a knife for this purpose. Put straight into boiling water with salt.

When the potatoes are cooked and drained and peeled (or peeled and cooked and drained, as the case may be), return them to the saucepan and over a low heat add a little milk, a good knob of butter or margarine, salt and pepper. Mash well with a fork or potato-masher. If you want to go to town over the job, add the yolk of an egg. Add more milk, very gradually, until the potatoes are creamy and smooth with no lumps at all. If you are fond of the FORCING-BAG, you can pipe them on to a heated dish; but personally I prefer them simply forked up on the dish and the sausages laid neatly across, with a sprig or two of parsley.

Fried or grilled tomatoes, bacon, fried onions, mushrooms, are all good GARNISHES, but some people just like sausages and mash and fresh mustard.

Remember to heat the meat dish and plates.

Spaghetti Alla Bolognese
(in Bologna style)

This is a dish which in a more comprehensive book would not be included under the heading Meat Dishes – but as we have no section for Italian PASTA, of which spaghetti is one of the many kinds, and as this method of serving it includes meat, we must stretch a point. If your only experience of spaghetti has been obtained from tins, this recipe will be a revelation to you.

A spaghetti party is an easy and popular kind of entertainment. You can make any amount of sauce the day before. As long as you have large enough vessels to cook the spaghetti in plenty of water, vast quantities can be cooked at a time in twenty minutes. Make sure you have sufficient large colanders to strain it.

Always buy genuine Italian spaghetti, which is long, or very long. The very long, about 22 in., may be broken in two before you cook it, to make it more manageable; but it should not be broken smaller.

Ingredients (to serve 4)

12 oz. spaghetti
1 small tin tomatoes (fresh tomatoes can be used, but this is one of the rare cases where the tinned product gives better results)
1 small onion
1 small CLOVE OF GARLIC (or a piece of one)
1½ oz. butter or margarine
1 rounded tablesp. tomato PURÉE, preferably Italian, available in tubes or tins, including a convenient very small size

1 oz. mushrooms
1½ tablesp. olive oil
2 tablesp. gravy (you can make this with a gravy cube)
1 bay leaf
4 oz. (or a little more) minced steak
3 or 4 oz. cheese for grating (Parmesan is best but expensive and the ready-grated tends to be tasteless; any hard cheese will do)

Utensils

1 large saucepan	Draining spoon
1 fairly heavy medium	Colander
saucepan	Cheese-grater
Wooden spoon	

Time required: 30–40 mins.

Method

1. Fill large saucepan two-thirds full of water, add 2 teasp. salt, and get it boiling fast.
2. Meanwhile, start your sauce: peel and chop onion and garlic fairly finely, wash and chop mushrooms coarsely.
3. Put spaghetti into fast-boiling water. Keep it moving by stirring occasionally with the draining-spoon. Cook for 12–15 mins. At the end of 12 mins. catch up a few 'strands' on the draining-spoon and pinch or bite them. When they are done they will be soft but still slightly resistant to pressure. (Undercooked, they will be like rubber; overcooked, they will be mushy.)
4. While the spaghetti is cooking, continue with the sauce: heat butter and oil in thick saucepan on low heat. Put in onions, garlic, mushrooms, and cook very gently for about 5 mins., stirring from time to time.
5. Now add tinned tomatoes, tomato PURÉE, bay leaf, and gravy. Stir well.
6. Add meat, stir, and cook very gently for 20 mins.
7. Grate cheese.
8. When spaghetti is cooked, drain – but not too thoroughly – into colander, and turn straight into a heated dish.
9. Give the sauce a final stir, taste, add pepper and salt as required, and pour over spaghetti.
10. Serve, with an ample supply of grated cheese handed separately.

It is best to use a somewhat deep dish for *spaghetti bolognese*, for although it is traditionally served with the sauce piled high on top of the *pasta*, unless there is room to mix it quite thoroughly at table before serving, the last-comers are apt to get all pasta and no sauce.

To offset the starchiness of *pasta* dishes, it is a good idea to serve a green salad, either with it on small separate plates, or afterwards as a separate course: lettuce or endive (alone or mixed), spring onions, watercress, mustard-and-cress, celery, chicory, or any other edible leaf including young dandelion leaves from the garden, and a good sharp French dressing (p. 112) with rather more vinegar than usual.

To eat spaghetti with a fork only, as the Italians do, requires practice. The alternative is to use a spoon in the left hand against which you lean the spaghetti-loaded prongs of the fork as you twiddle with the right.

Sausage Rolls, or Pasties

Sausage rolls are a commonplace and often disappointing form of food, but if you make them with FLAKY PASTRY or rough puff pastry and follow the suggestions below, they should be appetizing and satisfying. They can be served as an informal lunch or supper dish, when they should be piping hot and eaten with the fingers; or either hot or cold with a salad, or cold for a picnic. If they are to be eaten cold, make them small, so that the pastry is sure to be very crisp all through.

Made this way, they are always in great demand at parties. They really don't look at all like the conventional sausage roll, and would be better described as pasties.

Ingredients (to make 10 very small dainty pasties or 6 more solid ones)

For the rough puff pastry   6 oz. sausage-meat
(see p. 142):   1 rasher bacon (preferably
½ lb. plain flour   streaky)
Pinch salt   Small piece of onion

6 oz. fat (half margarine and   Salt and pepper
   half butter, or half lard and   Parsley
   half butter)   1 small egg
6–8 tablesp. cold water

Utensils

Strainer or flour-sieve   Scissors
Rolling-pin and pastry-board   2 cups
   (or clean table-top)   Fork
Sharp knife   Pastry brush
Chopping knife and board
2 basins, one medium, one
   rather large

Time required: To make pastry: about 1 hr, including
'rests' between rollings. When it is made, leave it for at least
15 mins. in refrigerator or cool place before using. To make
pasties: about 20 mins. To bake pasties: 20–25 mins.

Method

1. Set oven to Hot, Mark 8, 445° F.
2. Peel and chop onion finely. Chop parsley – about 1 teasp.
   Cut bacon into tiny pieces with scissors, discarding some
   of the fat if it is too fatty.
3. Put sausage-meat in basin, add onion, parsley, bacon,
   pepper, a little salt.
4. Break egg into cup. Pour off a little of the white into
   second cup and put aside.
5. Beat rest of egg and add half to sausage mixture. (Put
   rest aside for other use.) Mix all well. (This is best done
   with your hands, squeezing the somewhat stiff mixture
   through your fingers until everything is thoroughly
   incorporated.)
6. Roll out pastry to an oblong about 9 in. by 6 in. Cut into
   squares with sharp knife – as many as you require pasties.
7. Lay a small piece of sausage-meat in the centre of each
   square of pastry. Now fold opposite corners of each
   square over each other, moistening the top two with cold
   water to stick them together. Gently squeeze pasties into

envelopes longer than they are broad, or leave them as squares, whichever you prefer. They will look nicer on a dish if all are the same shape.

8. GLAZE the pastries with the pastry-brush dipped in the remaining white of egg.

9. Place on ungreased baking sheet and bake for 20–25 mins., when the pasties should be well risen and golden brown.

These sausage pasties will keep well in an airtight tin for several days in a cool place. They may be reheated on a wire tray or ovenproof dish at Warm, Mark 3, 335° F., for about 15 or 20 mins., or until crisp and hot right through.

Risotto

A risotto should be described as a rice dish rather than a meat dish, but as it frequently contains meat we include it here for want of a better place. It is an excellent dish in its own right, and also for stretching the remains of a chicken or using up the odd slice or two of ham. You can make a splendid risotto with chicken livers or a slice or two of calf's or other liver fried and cut into small pieces, in place of the chicken with which the following recipe is made. It is one of the easiest dishes to improvise; you can add or subtract almost anything, so long as the final result is really savoury, so some of the ingredients are marked 'optional'.

Ingredients (to serve 4)

2 oz. butter (plus ½ oz. to cook mushrooms)

1 large or 2 small rashers of bacon

1 small onion, or a piece of onion

1 small CLOVE OF GARLIC, or a piece (optional)

8 heaped tablesp. rice, Italian is best, otherwise Patna

About 4 heaped tablesp. cooked chicken meat cut rather small (or more if liked)

1 pt (approx.) good STOCK,
or equivalent in chicken
soup cubes. (It is difficult
to give the exact amount
of stock, as some rices
absorb more liquid than
others. You can always
make a little more by
quickly dissolving part of
a soup cube in hot water.)
1–2 oz. mushrooms (optional)
Pepper and salt
2 oz. cheese for grating

Utensils

2 medium saucepans (one of
which should be fairly
heavy)
Wooden spoon
Knife
Scissors
1 small saucepan
Clean cloth
Strainer
Cheese-grater

Time required: About ¾ hr

Method

1. Peel and chop garlic finely. Peel and chop onion coarsely
(you may DICE it if you like). Cut up bacon rashers with
scissors – pieces about the size of half a stamp. If the
rashers are fatty, put some of the fat aside for frying the
mushrooms (if you are using them). In any case, don't
put too much fat in the risotto.
2. Melt 2 oz. butter in heavy pan. Put in garlic, onion, and
bacon; fry very gently, stirring with wooden spoon, for
about 3 mins.
3. Meanwhile put rice in strainer and run cold water on it,
shaking it about to wash it well. Shake off surplus water.
4. Add washed rice to other ingredients in pan and fry all
very gently for another minute or two.
5. In the meantime, heat STOCK (or chicken soup cubes and
water) almost to boiling point.
6. Remove pan with rice, etc., from heat and pour on about
a third of the hot STOCK, stirring well. Return pan to
heat and continue to cook a little faster until all the stock
has been absorbed by the rice. Keep the rest of the stock
hot.

7. Add more STOCK, a little at a time, as it is absorbed. Some rices take up more liquid than others. The rice will absorb all it can in from 20 to 30 mins. Test it by biting a grain or two to see if it is soft right through. If there is still a hard core, add a little more hot STOCK. The cooked rice should be soft but not mushy. Taste, and add pepper and salt as required. Remember that some soup cubes, if used, tend to be very salty.

8. While the rice is cooking, remove all the chicken from the bones and cut up the amount you require into small pieces.

9. If you are using mushrooms, wash and dry these (do not peel them), cut up – stalks and all – into fairly small pieces. Melt $\frac{1}{2}$ oz. butter in small pan, add any bacon fat and the chopped mushrooms, and cook gently for about 5 mins.

10. When rice is quite soft, add the cut-up chicken and stir well. CORRECT SEASONING. Add mushrooms last of all.

11. Turn the risotto into a heated dish – preferably a deep one, so that second helpings will not get cold. (Cold risotto is horrid.)

12. Hand grated cheese, which should be liberally sprinkled over each helping.

Serve a salad as well.

Plain Boiled Rice
(for Stews, Curries, etc.)

It is very necessary to know how to cook rice properly. It is served as an accompaniment to many dishes instead of potatoes, and should be dry and hot, with every grain separate from the others, instead of the soggy, gelatinous mess so often produced.

Allow 2 oz. or 2 heaped tablesp. per person. (Any rice left over can be used to make Spanish salad.) Long-grain rice is best as an accompaniment to savoury dishes.

Ingredients

Patna or other long-grain rice,
  2 oz. per person
NUT of butter

·Salt, about 1 level teasp. for
  every 2 oz.

Utensils

Large saucepan (rice swells
  enormously in the cooking,
  and must have plenty of
  water – about 1½ pts to each
  2 oz. – to take up some of the
  starch)

Spoon
Strainer
Fork

Time required: 15 mins. (or more)

Method

1. Have pan ready with fast-boiling water. Add salt.
2. Rinse rice in strainer under running cold water.
3. Pour slowly into boiling water. Stir once or twice.
4. Boil fast for 15 mins. or until cooked, i.e. soft but still firm.
5. Meanwhile have a dish warming in the oven with a NUT of butter.
6. Have a kettle of boiling water ready.
7. Test rice by pinching or biting a few grains. When it is cooked (see 4), turn it into strainer.
8. Hold strainer over sink and pour boiling water slowly over rice to separate grains. Shake, and turn into hot dish.
9. Fork it about in the butter, to separate grains again. If possible, leave to dry a little in oven for about 10 mins. before serving.

A Few Sauces

The sauces required for good everyday cookery are not difficult (I don't refer to the works of art used in fine French cooking) but require care. The sauce can make or mar the dish.

One of the first things to learn is how to make a white sauce, on which a number of other sauces are based.

Basic White Sauce
(to make 1 pt)

This can be made thin (pouring), thick (coating), or very thick (PANADA or binding), according to the purpose for which it is needed.

Ingredients

Thin: 1½ oz. flour
1½ oz. butter
1 pt milk
Thick: 2 oz. flour
2 oz. butter
1 pt milk

Very Thick: 3 oz. flour
3 oz. butter
1 pt milk

For a savoury sauce, add salt and pepper; for a sweet sauce, sugar or other ingredients according to recipe.

Utensils

Small thick saucepan
Wooden spoon

Time required: 10 mins.

Method

1. Make a ROUX by melting butter in saucepan over low heat, stirring in flour as it melts. Cook gently for 2 mins., stirring all the time.
2. Remove pan from heat and add a little of the milk – which may be cold, warm, or hot, but not boiling. Stir.
3. Replace on heat, add rest of milk slowly, stirring constantly until it comes to the boil.
4. Boil very gently for 5 mins., stirring often, to produce a smooth velvety sauce.
5. Add seasonings as required by recipe.
6. If the sauce is in the least lumpy, strain and reheat.

(Any sauce made with flour should be cooked for at least 5 mins.)

Cheese Sauce

Ingredients (to make 1 pt)

1½ oz. flour
1½ oz. butter ⎫ for thin white
1 pt milk ⎭ sauce
3–4 oz. cheese for grating

Salt and pepper
1 teasp. French mustard
(optional)

T–E

Utensils

1 small thick saucepan   Cheese-grater
Wooden spoon

Time required: 15 mins.

Method

1. Grate cheese.
2. Make 1 pt white sauce.
3. Add mustard (if used). Add cheese. Heat just long enough for the cheese to melt. Taste, and season with salt and pepper. The sauce should not boil after cheese is added, or cheese will become tough and indigestible.

Parsley Sauce

Make a thin white sauce (or thick if you prefer), and add plenty of chopped parsley.

Tomato Sauce

Ingredients (to make a good ½ pt)

1 lb. tomatoes or 1 small tin of tomatoes; or about 2 heaped tablesp. from a tube or tin of concentrated tomato PURÉE made up to ½ pt with water

¼ pt STOCK (or use meat extract or gravy cube with water)

1½ oz. butter or margarine

1½ oz. flour

A small bay-leaf (or a piece of one)

1 medium-size onion

1 CLOVE OF GARLIC (optional)

Pinch of sugar

Salt and pepper

2 or 3 bacon rinds

Utensils

Chopping knife and board	Wooden spoon
2 small saucepans	Sieve or strainer
Knife	Basin

Time required: About $\frac{3}{4}$ hr

Method

1. Peel and chop onion fairly fine (also garlic, if using). If fresh tomatoes are to be used, wash and slice them thickly.
2. Heat butter or margarine in saucepan and MELT onions (and garlic), together with bacon rinds, for 3 or 4 mins.
3. Stir flour into softened onions with wooden spoon, and cook gently, stirring constantly, for 1 or 2 mins.
4. Remove from heat and add stock (warm or cold, but not boiling), stirring well.
5. Return to heat. Add tomatoes with bay leaf. Cover and SIMMER 20 mins. if using fresh tomatoes; 10 mins. if using tinned tomatoes; 5 mins. if using PURÉE.
6. Rub through sieve or strainer into basin, first removing bay leaf.
7. Return to saucepan. Add salt, pepper, a pinch of sugar. Bring to boiling point and simmer for another two or three minutes. CORRECT SEASONING.

If you want a rather sharper sauce, you may add 1 or 2 teasp. vinegar at the end. Some people like a pinch of powdered MACE.

Mayonnaise

I have made mayonnaise many a time with just a wooden spoon and a soup-plate to beat it in – and if you have no beater or whisk this is the easiest way to go about it, as the shallow plate allows plenty of air to get to the mixture.

If you have a ROTARY BEATER or wire egg-whisk, use a

bowl rather than a plate. If you have an electric mixer, follow the directions that come with it, which usually require you to use the white as well as the yolk of egg.

The point to remember is: never lose patience and start to drop the oil in fast before you have reached the point where the mayonnaise has really begun to thicken. If you do, you may *never* reach this point. Also in cold weather bring the oil into a warm room well before you are ready to use it; cold oil may curdle the mayonnaise.

Mayonnaise should not be kept in a refrigerator, where the ingredients tend to separate, but will keep for several weeks in a cool larder (except in a heat-wave). Because making it is a somewhat tedious job, it is advisable to make a double quantity each time and put half aside. Making a lot takes very little longer than making a little: it is the first half of the operation which is slow.

The following recipe makes a good ¼ pt of mayonnaise – sufficient for a potato salad for four.

Ingredients

¼ pt olive oil or other salad oil
1 egg yolk
1½ dessertsp. vinegar (WINE VINEGAR is best)

½ level teasp. dry mustard
1 level teasp. salt
Pinch of pepper

Utensils

Medium basin
Rotary beater or egg whisk

or simply a wooden spoon and a deep plate

Time required: About 20 mins.

Method

1. Put egg yolk, mustard, salt, pepper, and 1 dessertsp. vinegar in a basin, and beat.
2. Now begin to add the oil, *two or three drops at a time,*

beating constantly and blending well before adding more. When about a third of the oil is in, you may add the rest more quickly; but don't overdo it.

3. Add the rest of the vinegar, beating it in thoroughly.
4. (Should the mayonnaise curdle or fail to thicken, put another egg yolk in a clean basin and beat the mayonnaise into this, a very little at a time. If this doesn't work, nothing will. You can eat the concoction you have produced, but it won't be mayonnaise.)

If you want a very rich mayonnaise for a special dish – chicken mayonnaise for a party, for instance – add cream last of all, a little at a time, tasting as you go.

Sauce Tartare
(for Fried Fish or Grilled Meat)

Ingredients (to make ¼ pt)

¼ pt MAYONNAISE
Small piece of onion
1 teasp. parsley

2 or 3 gherkins *or* 1 tablesp. CAPERS, plus in either case 1 teasp. of their liquor

Utensils

As for MAYONNAISE
Chopping knife and board

Parsley-mincer

Time required: About 25–30 mins.

Method

1. Make MAYONNAISE (see p. 109).
2. Peel and chop onion finely, chop gherkins or CAPERS fairly finely, mince parsley.
3. Add these to MAYONNAISE, add 1 teasp. of liquor from gherkins or CAPERS, mix well.

Serve in SAUCE-BOAT with ladle.

French Dressing

A French dressing, which is the simplest and best dressing for most salads, is made with oil and vinegar in the proportions of three parts of oil to one of vinegar. (Sometimes less vinegar is used, but personally I often find it preferable to use a little more; you must taste, and judge for yourself.) To this are added salt, pepper, and sometimes a pinch of dry mustard. There are some who add a pinch of sugar; but again you must decide for yourself.

Use WINE VINEGAR rather than malt vinegar, when you can. Olive oil is always good, but try cheaper salad oils too. TARRAGON VINEGAR or other herb-flavoured vinegars are nice for a change. Use freshly ground pepper from a mill if possible.

The dressing can be made in fairly large quantities in advance and kept in a corked or screw-top bottle or jar, which must be well shaken before use, as vinegar and oil will separate; but the best way to dress a salad is described under Green Salad, p. 57.

Custard Sauce
(for Puddings, Stewed Fruit, etc.)

Ingredients (to make 1 pt custard)

1 pt milk	A few drops of VANILLA or
2 eggs	other flavouring (rum, for
1 tablesp. sugar	instance)

Utensils

DOUBLE SAUCEPAN *or*	Fork
BAIN-MARIE	Tablespoon
Wooden spoon	Strainer

Time required: 15–20 mins.

Method

1. Beat eggs lightly, enough to mix well.
2. Pour on milk, add sugar.
3. Cook over boiling water, in DOUBLE SAUCEPAN or BAIN-MARIE, stirring constantly, until custard thickens and coats back of wooden spoon. At this stage, remove at once from heat or the custard will curdle.
4. Strain into jug, add flavouring, and stir well.

As a nation, we are addicted to custard on practically everything which turns up as a sweet course. A true egg custard is far nicer than using custard powder from a tin and, if you make it often, it is well worth while having VANILLA SUGAR to hand. You make this by buying a VANILLA POD and keeping it in a jar with a pound or two of sugar, regularly replenished. It gives the custard or other sweets a finer flavour than bottled VANILLA ESSENCE.

Chocolate Sauce

This can be used, hot or cold, for a great many puddings and sweets, soufflés, sponges, *Poire Hélène*, etc.

Ingredients (to make about ½ pt)

2 oz. plain chocolate (cooking or dessert)
½ pt water
2 oz. sugar (or more, if you like it very sweet)

2 level teasp. ARROWROOT
½ teasp. VANILLA ESSENCE
or use VANILLA SUGAR

Utensils

Small saucepan
Teaspoon

Wooden spoon
Grater

Time required: 10 mins.

Method

1. Grate chocolate into saucepan.
2. Add sugar and ARROWROOT, and mix smoothly with a little of the water.
3. Add rest of water, and bring to boiling point, stirring constantly. SIMMER 5 mins., stirring occasionally.
4. Add vanilla (if using).

Serve hot or cold. Other flavourings may be used – 1 tablesp. rum, or a few drops of rum essence, or orange essence, or orange liqueur.

Hot Puddings and Cold Sweets

Orleans Pudding

This light pudding has a strong blackcurrant flavour.

Ingredients (to serve 5 or 6)

6 oz. self-raising flour
2 oz. caster sugar
4 oz. butter or margarine
2 eggs
Pinch of salt

½ level teasp. bicarbonate of
    soda
1 dessertsp. milk
4–5 rounded tablesp.
    blackcurrant jam

Utensils

Steamer *or* large saucepan
  and medium basin for
   BAIN-MARIE
Another medium basin
1 small basin
1 large basin
Wooden spoon

Small saucepan
Sieve or strainer
Greaseproof paper or
  aluminium foil
Scissors
Tablespoon

Time required: About 1¾ hrs

Method

1. Thoroughly grease medium basin with butter. Cut piece of greaseproof or foil somewhat larger than top of basin and grease one side well.

2. CREAM butter and sugar in large basin with wooden spoon.

3. Add eggs, one at a time, beating each in thoroughly before adding next.

4. Add jam.

5. Sieve flour with salt over second medium basin, and add to rest of mixture, stirring in well with metal spoon.

6. Warm dessertsp. milk. Dissolve bicarb. in it and add to mixture, stirring well.

7. Turn mixture into greased basin. It should not be more than three-quarters full, to allow for rising.

8. Cover top of basin with greased paper or foil, greased side down. If using foil, twist the edges under rim of basin; greaseproof paper must be tied round with string.

9. Steam in top half of steamer with plenty of water boiling below, or in a BAIN-MARIE, for 1¼ hrs.

10. Warm a little more blackcurrant jam by standing the jar in a small saucepan of warm water, bringing to the boil, and boiling gently for 10 mins.

11. To turn out, run a knife round edge of pudding (after removing paper, of course) and turn basin upside down on to heated serving plate. A gentle shake should bring

the pudding out unbroken. To be extra sure of this, leave it for a few minutes before attempting to turn out.

12. Put a little more blackcurrant jam on top of pudding and serve.

Don't be surprised if the pudding has a greenish tinge. It hasn't gone mouldy – the blackcurrants do this.

Hot Chocolate Soufflé

This need not be considered as a 'special occasion' sweet; it is perfectly simple to make. Serve it with hot chocolate sauce (see p. 113) flavoured with a little rum if you have it or rum essence if you haven't.

For general hints on soufflé making, read paragraphs 1 and 3 of the recipe for cheese soufflé (see p. 36). The basic method is similar for all SOUFFLÉS, but for the sake of clarity I repeat it below.

Ingredients (to serve 4–6)

1 oz. butter
1 oz. caster sugar
1 oz. plain flour
¼ pt milk
4 eggs (i.e. 3 plus 1 extra white)

½ teasp. VANILLA ESSENCE
2 oz. *plain* chocolate, either cooking or dessert
Butter for greasing

Utensils

SOUFFLÉ DISH or round ovenware casserole (see note under 'Utensils', p. 37) medium size, i.e. about 6 in. base
2 medium basins
Small/medium solid saucepan
Small saucepan

Wooden spoon
Tablespoon
Cup
Grater
Scissors
Pastry-brush
Pin
Greaseproof paper
Egg-whisk

Time required: ¾–1 hr

Method

1. Set oven to Fairly Hot, Mark 6, 400° F.
2. Melt 1 teasp. butter in small saucepan and grease
   SOUFFLÉ DISH thoroughly, using pastry-brush. Cut a
   strip of greaseproof paper long enough to go right round
   dish with slight overlap, and deep enough to come 2 in.
   above edge. Grease this well too and pin it round the
   outside of dish, greased side inwards.
3. Grate chocolate into small saucepan, pour on a little of
   the milk, and stir over low heat until chocolate is dissolved. Then add rest of milk, stir well, remove from
   heat.
4. Now make PANADA. Melt butter in larger saucepan,
   stir in flour smoothly, cook for one or two minutes over
   low heat, stirring constantly. Then gradually add milk
   and chocolate, continuing to stir until mixture thickens
   and leaves sides of pan clean. Remove from heat. Beat
   in sugar and vanilla.
5. Take 3 eggs and SEPARATE them (one at a time),
   putting yolks in one basin and whites in another. Add
   yolks to mixture, one at a time, beating each in
   thoroughly.
6. Break the fourth egg, setting yolk aside in cup and adding
   white to other whites. (The yolk can be kept in a cool
   place and used for MAYONNAISE or custards, to add to
   mashed potato, etc.) Whisk up the four whites until stiff
   enough to stand up.
7. FOLD stiff whites into mixture in saucepan, making sure
   to get your spoon right down to the bottom of the
   mixture.
8. Turn into prepared dish and bake for about 30 mins.
   Remove paper collar and serve at once.

You can bake this mixture in individual SOUFFLÉ DISHES or
paper cases. In this case no paper collar is required, but fill
the cases only three parts full and bake in a hotter oven for
about 15 mins.

(Soufflés can also be steamed.)

Sweet Omelette

An omelette can be served with jam or other sweet filling, as a pudding, but is then best made as a soufflé omelette instead of the more usual way.

Soufflé Omelette with Jam

Ingredients (to serve 2)

3 eggs
2 tablesp. water
1 oz. butter

1 or 2 rounded tablesp. jam
2 level teasp. caster sugar

Utensils

Omelette-pan
Small saucepan
SPATULA
Fork

2 medium basins
Egg-whisk
Tablespoon

Time required: 25–30 mins.

Method

1. Warm jam by standing jar or cup of jam in saucepan of warm water, bringing to boil, and SIMMERING gently until omelette is ready.

2. Break eggs and SEPARATE YOLKS FROM WHITES in 2 bowls.

3. Whisk yolks thoroughly until pale and frothy. Add sugar and water (which should be warm) and whisk again.

4. Rinse the whisk until it is quite clean, under cold water. Now whisk whites of egg until they are so stiff that you can reverse the basin without their falling out. (Take care when trying it.)

5. Melt butter in pan over low heat. (If you have heat too high, omelette will rise rapidly and collapse equally rapidly.)

6. FOLD egg whites gently into yolks. Turn on grill at moderately low heat.

7. Turn mixture into pan, turn up heat a very little, and cook until omelette is lightly browned underneath and beginning to rise – about 5 mins.

8. Place pan beneath grill until omelette is dry on top – about 8 mins. or a little more.

9. With spatula, SCORE omelette down centre, spoon in 1 or 2 tablesp. hot jam, and fold omelette over. If necessary, loosen round edges and ease from pan on to hot dish with spatula.

Serve at once.

(A soufflé omelette may also be filled with any savoury filling.)

Jam Puffs

These are good hot as a pudding, and can also be eaten cold as tea-time pastry.

Ingredients (to make 6, 9, or 12 puffs according to size of cutters)

½ lb. puff pastry (see p. 142)   Milk or egg white
Jam

Utensils

2 pastry-cutters, one ½ in.   Teaspoon
   smaller than the other   Baking sheet
Pastry-brush   Knife
Small saucepan

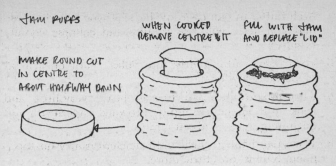

JAM PUFFS

WHEN COOKED
REMOVE CENTRE BIT

FILL WITH JAM
AND REPLACE "LID"

MAKE ROUND CUT
IN CENTRE TO
ABOUT HALFWAY DOWN

Time required: To make pastry: About 2 hrs including 'rests'. To make and bake: 30–40 mins.

Method

1. Set oven to Hot, Mark 8, 445° F.

2. Roll out pastry to just under $\frac{1}{4}$ in. thick.

3. Cut as many rings as possible with larger cutter. (It helps to prevent sticking if cutter is dipped in flour each time.) With smaller cutter, cut a ring in the centre of each large ring, *almost but not quite through to the bottom*. Do not remove this ring, but withdraw the cutter carefully, easing the pastry off with your finger.

4. GLAZE the top of each with a little milk or white of egg.

5. Place puffs on ungreased baking sheet, not too close together, and bake on second shelf from top of oven for about 20 mins. or until they are well risen and golden brown.

6. Remove baking sheet from oven. Lift off the top from each puff with help of a knife, and lay it upside-down on baking sheet. Turn oven down to Warm, Mark 3, 335° F.

Replace baking sheet. Allow puffs to dry out for 5–10 mins.

7. Meanwhile, heat jam by standing jar or cup of jam in small saucepan of warm water, bringing to boil and SIMMERING gently for 10 mins. or until puffs are ready.

8. Remove puffs from oven, and if there is any soft, un-cooked pastry still inside, scoop it out with teaspoon and throw away. Fill puffs with hot jam, replace 'lids', and serve.

If the puffs are wanted cold, allow them to cool on a wire tray before filling with cold jam. A blob of whipped cream on top of the jam is delicious.

VOL-AU-VENTS (see p. 218) are made in the same way and filled with a savoury filling of shrimps or mushrooms, etc., in a fairly thick white sauce, preferably with cream added to it.

Castle Puddings

This is a very quick, light pudding and usually much appreciated. In the note about a basic sponge mixture in the recipe for Sultana Sponge Cakes (see p. 149), you will find the formula (the weight of the eggs in sugar, fat, and flour).

It is a good idea to make double the quantity of the mixture and bake a small batch of little cakes or a sponge sandwich at the same time. You can even eat the Castle Puddings cold, as cakes; or you can bake the mixture in one mould or ovenware basin (20–30 mins. baking time). If you don't want to use the oven, you can steam the mixture (see recipe for Orleans Pudding, p. 115), but this takes longer.

Ingredients (to serve 6)

2 eggs
The weight of the eggs in

Butter or lard for greasing
    moulds

sugar, butter or margarine, and self-raising flour

Pinch of salt

Few drops VANILLA ESSENCE (or use VANILLA SUGAR in place of ordinary sugar)

1 teasp. each flour and caster sugar for dusting moulds

Jam

Desiccated coconut (optional)

Utensils

6–8 DARIOLE MOULDS or other small metal or ovenware moulds

Baking sheet

2 medium basins

Small saucepan

Wooden spoon

Tablespoon

Teaspoon

Fork

Sieve or strainer

Piece of paper

Time required: About ½ hr

Method

1. Set oven to Fairly Hot, Mark 6, 400° F.
2. Thoroughly grease moulds. Mix teasp. flour and teasp. caster sugar on piece of paper and sprinkle a little inside each mould, turning them so that they are lined with the mixture. A gentle tap on the bottom of one over another will remove surplus without wasting any.
3. Warm basin for a minute at bottom of oven. Put in sugar and butter (or marg.) and CREAM them well.
4. Break in one egg, beat in thoroughly with wooden spoon. Repeat with other egg. Beat until mixture is light and creamy and sugar almost dissolved.
5. Mix flour and salt and sift into second basin.
6. Add this to egg mixture, a little at a time, stirring in thoroughly. Add VANILLA ESSENCE if using. If mixture is at all stiff, add a few drops of cold water.
7. Fill moulds not more than two-thirds full, stand on baking sheet, and bake on second shelf from top of oven for 10–15 mins.
8. Meanwhile, warm jam by standing jar or cup of jam in

small saucepan of warm water, bringing to boil, and SIMMERING gently until puddings are cooked.

9. When cooked (test by inserting skewer into one; if it comes out clean, they are cooked. Or press gently with finger; if sponge is done, the impression will spring back.), remove from oven and allow to cool for 2 or 3 mins.

10. When puddings have shrunk a little from the sides of the moulds, turn them out on to a hot dish. If they stick at all, run a knife round the edges.

11. Spoon a little hot jam (or a lot) over each castle and sprinkle with desiccated coconut if liked. Some people put a GLACÉ CHERRY on top.

Apple Pudding

This pudding (sometimes known as Friar's Omelette) is a useful one to know when cooking apples become cheap and plentiful or when the ground is strewn with windfalls.

Ingredients (to serve 6)

About 2 lb. cooking apples (preferably Bramleys or another quick-cooking kind)
3 oz. butter
3 oz. demerara sugar

2 eggs
1 or 2 oz. sultanas, to taste
Large pinch CINNAMON
3 oz. fresh BREADCRUMBS
Butter for greasing

Utensils

Knife
Wooden spoon
Fork
Small basin

Medium saucepan
Pie-dish
Grater
Strainer

Time required: $1\frac{1}{4}$–$1\frac{1}{2}$ hrs

Method

1. Peel apples, cut into quarters, remove core, and cut each quarter into 2 or 3 slices.

2. Put in saucepan with butter and sugar and stew very slowly, stirring often with wooden spoon. No water should be needed, but if apples show any tendency to stick to pan, add a very little water.

3. When quite soft, remove from heat, beat a little with fork to ensure there are no lumps, and leave to get nearly cold.

4. Meanwhile, beat eggs well in small basin.

5. Grease pie-dish well with butter. Set oven to Moderate, Mark 4, 355° F.

6. Make breadcrumbs and pour two-thirds of these into pie-dish, turning it around so that all sides become thickly coated with crumbs.

7. Wash sultanas in strainer under running water, and drain.

8. When apple is nearly cold, stir in beaten eggs, CINNA-MON, and sultanas.

9. Turn mixture into pie-dish, cover with remainder of BREADCRUMBS.

10. Bake for 30 mins. Turn out carefully on to hot plate.

Serve with cream if possible.

Chocolate Mousse

This is one of the most useful recipes I know. It is very easily made, quite delicious, suitable either for a family treat or for the most formal meal, and not wildly extravagant. It is best served in small individual dishes or glasses (little SOUFFLÉ DISHES are perfect). For parties, it may be served in small oiled-paper cases and made well in advance. It is rather rich, so no one needs a large helping.

Ingredients (to serve 4 or 5)

3 oz. good cooking chocolate (or any plain chocolate)

3 eggs
1 tablesp. rum (optional)

Utensils

A DOUBLE SAUCEPAN or a
saucepan with a basin
which will stand comfortably
inside it, a BAIN-MARIE)
2 more medium-size basins

Egg-whisk or ROTARY
BEATER
Wooden spoon
Metal spoon
Knife

Time required: 15 mins.

Method

1. Cut chocolate into small pieces and place in top half of DOUBLE SAUCEPAN or use BAIN-MARIE. Fill lower half of saucepan with water. Heat fairly fast until water is boiling and chocolate melts.

2. Break the eggs into two bowls, SEPARATING WHITES FROM YOLKS.

3. Whisk up whites of egg stiffly. They should be stiff enough to hold any shape you push them into.

4. Remove chocolate from heat, and stir in yolks one by one with wooden spoon.

5. Gently FOLD whites into chocolate mixture until it is well mixed.

6. Pour into individual dishes and serve as cold as possible.

For a special occasion, you may make this sweet even more luscious by adding a little cream to the mixture before you fold in the white of egg, or by putting a large blob of WHIPPED CREAM on top of each dish, or both. A tablespoon of rum may be added at the same stage.

Crème Caramel
(Caramel Custard)

There are two methods of doing this. The recipe for the custard is the same in each, but the caramel is made differently. The first is the most usual, but the caramel is a little difficult to handle. The second method is unorthodox, but I recommend it.

Ingredients (to make 8 individual custards or 1 large one)

1. CONVENTIONAL METHOD

Custard:

4 fresh eggs
1 pt milk
2 level tablesp. sugar
Few drops vanilla essence (or
   use VANILLA SUGAR instead
   of plain sugar)
Butter for greasing

Caramel:

4½ level tablesp. granulated
   or caster sugar
3 tablesp. water

Utensils

8 small ovenproof dishes or
   1 large one, to take 1½ pts
   liquid easily (SOUFFLÉ
   DISHES are ideal)
Strainer
Baking tin

Fork
Tablespoon
1 large jug
1 fairly large basin
1 cup
1 very small saucepan

Time required: To make: About 25 mins. To cook: 1–1½ hrs, according to size and depth of baking dishes.

Method

The Caramel

NOTE: Burnt sugar is *not* caramel!

1. Put sugar and water together into small pan and boil gently but steadily, stirring occasionally with metal spoon, for about 5 to 8 or 9 mins. (caster sugar caramelizes more quickly than granulated), until a rich, reddish-brown syrup is produced. Watch it very carefully towards the end of the time and remove pan from heat the moment the colour is deep enough, as it will continue to cook and darken for several moments after it is removed. (If the sugar turns very dark, it will be

bitter and you will have to throw it away and start again.)

2. While this is going on, grease dishes or dish in which you are going to bake the custard. A butter wrapping-paper (not margarine, which is not a good greasing agent) or any piece of clean paper with a scrap of butter does this job.

3. Immediately the caramel is dark enough, pour a little caramel straight from the pan into the greased dishes and turn the dish about so that the bottom and about $\frac{1}{4}$ in. up the sides are coated. If using small dishes, don't be too lavish with the first ones, or you will not have sufficient to go round, and as the caramel sets hard at once, you cannot pour from one to the other later on. (This is one reason for my preference for the second method.)

The Custard

1. Break eggs first into cup to test their freshness, then turn into jug, add sugar, and beat just enough to break up eggs. Now pour on milk.

2. Add 2 or 3 drops VANILLA ESSENCE (unless using VANILLA SUGAR). Beat again to mix, but not too much.

3. Pour through strainer into basin to trap the 'eyes' of the eggs. Pour strained custard back into jug.

4. Fill dish or dishes, which are already coated with caramel.

5. Stand dish or dishes in baking tin and fill tin with warm water to come half-way up sides of dishes.

6. Bake in centre or low in oven at Moderate, Mark 3, 335° F. The water in the tin must not boil or the custards will have holes in them when set.

Allow to get cold. It is preferable not to try to turn out a large custard, which will almost certainly break. To turn out individual custards, run a thin knife round the edges, place a small dish on top of the custard, and reverse both dishes quickly. A slight shake should bring the custard out, nicely coated with caramel.

2. RECOMMENDED METHOD

A more liquid form of caramel, which tastes equally good and is easier to handle, can be made as described below. The great advantage of this is that, although it does not set hard (and will therefore not coat the mould at the time it is poured in as neatly as the usual kind of caramel), it can be made in any quantity, bottled, and kept for use at any time. Not only caramel custard but rice pudding and other milk puddings, hot or cold, junkets, and even stewed apples are given a new interest by the addition of a little caramel.

In making caramel this way, exact quantities are not important; but use a little more sugar in relation to the water, to allow for a small quantity sticking to the spoon.

Ingredients

5 level tablesp. granulated   3 tablesp. water
   or caster sugar

Utensils

As above plus another small
   saucepan

Method

1. Put sugar into small saucepan on lowest heat. It will begin to melt and then to brown. Shake the pan from time to time, or stir with metal spoon. Caster sugar will colour faster than granulated. A small quantity will take 5 mins. or less to go a deep reddish-brown; more will take longer.

2. Heat a little water to boiling point in second pan.

3. Remove sugar from heat immediately it is sufficiently coloured (do not let it get too dark), and spoon in slowly and carefully the 3 tablesp. boiling water, stirring each tablesp. well in. *The sugar may spit, so be careful.*

4. When sugar and water are well mixed, return pan to heat for a few minutes, stirring well, especially around the edges of the pan, where sugar is apt to stick. Don't worry if a little remains on spoon.

5. Pour a little into each greased dish.

Make custard exactly as before. When you pour it into the dishes, the caramel, being liquid, will tend to mix with the custard. But if the operation is gently done, only a little will mix, hardly altering the colour of the custard; and when turned out, the custards will be coated at the base and surrounded by a small pool of delicious liquid caramel.

Gooseberry Fool

Ingredients (to serve 6)

1 lb. gooseberries
½ gill (⅛ pt) water
3 or 4 level tablesp. sugar
Green colouring
2 whites of egg

Custard
½ pt milk
2 eggs
1 level tablesp. sugar
A little cream (optional)

Utensils

1 medium saucepan
Measuring jug
Tablespoon
DOUBLE SAUCEPAN or
  BAIN-MARIE

Wooden spoon
Egg whisk or ROTARY
  BEATER
Fine sieve or strainer
Basin

Time required: about 30 mins.

Method

1. Wash gooseberries and stew gently in saucepan with water and sugar for about 10–15 mins., or until soft.
2. Meanwhile, make custard: Beat 2 eggs lightly, pour on milk, add sugar, and cook in DOUBLE SAUCEPAN or BAIN-MARIE, stirring constantly, for about 20 mins., or until custard thickens and coats back of wooden spoon. Remove at once from heat.
3. Put cooked gooseberries through fine strainer with wooden spoon. You now have a PURÉE in your bowl.

4. Stir custard into PURÉE. Mix well, taste, and add more sugar if necessary.

5. If using cream, add at this stage.

6. Whisk up two egg whites until stiff; FOLD into mixture.

7. When mixture is smooth and creamy, add two or three drops of green colouring. Be very careful not to add too much. The final colour should be a *delicate* green.

8. Chill thoroughly, before serving in a glass dish or individual glasses.

A rhubarb fool can be made the same way, but can be put through a much coarser sieve, or, if it is young and tender, simply whipped with a fork. Or cooked rhubarb can be liquidized with the other ingredients in an electric liquidizer. Gooseberries *must* be put through a sieve to eliminate the pips.

Honeycomb Mould

This is a simple sweet which children usually love.

Ingredients (to serve 6)

1 pt milk (slightly less if you have no refrigerator in which to set the sweet)

1 jelly of any flavour (the lighter colours look more attractive)

¼ gill water (1 gill = ¼ pt)
2 level tablesp. sugar
3 eggs

Utensils

1 medium saucepan
1 small saucepan
2 medium basins
Fork

Wooden spoon
Strainer
ROTARY BEATER or egg whisk
Jelly mould

Time required: About ¾ hr plus time to set (approximately 1½ hrs in refrigerator, or several hrs or overnight without one).

Method

1. Break eggs carefully, SEPARATING WHITES FROM YOLKS, into the two basins.
2. Beat up yolks of eggs with sugar.
3. Bring milk to boil in saucepan.
4. Pour milk slowly on to yolks and sugar, stirring constantly. Return to pan, and stir over low heat with wooden spoon until mixture thickens. This custard must not be allowed to boil, so stir steadily and do not relax your attention. When it is thick enough to coat back of wooden spoon – 5–10 mins. – remove from heat and allow to cool.
5. Melt jelly in the water in small saucepan over very low heat, stirring a little.
6. When custard is cool, strain jelly into it, stirring well. Stir often until nearly cold.
7. Meanwhile, whip whites of eggs to stiff froth. They should hold any shape you push them into. When custard is nearly cold, FOLD in the stiffly beaten whites.
8. Rinse out mould in cold water and pour mixture in. Leave to set in refrigerator or cool larder.

To turn out, stand mould up to its edge in a basin of very hot water for a few moments, then reverse on to dish and give a sharp shake.

Poire Hélène

This is a delectable sweet for special occasions. You can make a quick imitation of it by using tinned halves of pears, but to my mind these are always insipid in flavour. It is perfectly permissible to use a good brand of commercial ice-cream, but if you have a refrigerator and would like to make your own, you will find a recipe in this section.

Ingredients (to serve 4)

4 good dessert pears of even
 size
¼ pt water
2 oz. sugar
A vanilla pod (or ½ teasp.
 VANILLA ESSENCE)

½ pt (or a little less) hot
 chocolate sauce (see p.
 113)
4 portions vanilla ice-cream

Utensils

1 thick saucepan with lid
 (just large enough to allow
 pears to lie flat)
1 small saucepan

Knife
Tablespoon
Individual dishes for serving
Utensils to make sauce

Time required: About 30 mins. plus time for pears to
become quite cold.

Method

1. Put sugar, water, and VANILLA POD (or ESSENCE) in
   small saucepan and bring to boil.

2. Meanwhile, peel pears thinly, leaving stalks on, and lay
   side by side in saucepan.

3. Pour boiling syrup over (leave VANILLA POD in), cover,
   and cook very gently – turning pears once, with care
   not to damage them – for about 15 mins. Remove from
   heat and allow to get quite cold in syrup. Then remove
   VANILLA POD (which may be washed, dried, and re-
   used a number of times).

4. Make chocolate sauce before serving first course (it takes
   10 mins.) and keep hot in a BAIN-MARIE, or reheat
   quickly before needed. It must be at boiling point when
   served.

5. To serve, put a helping of ice-cream in each dish, making
   an impression in centre with back of spoon. Place a pear
   upright in the impression and pour a little syrup over.
   Bring the boiling hot sauce to table in an attractive jug

and pour some over as you hand each dish. Both pears and ice-cream should be well coated with sauce.

Vanilla Ice-cream

Ice-cream made at home in the refrigerator can be delicious, and is certainly more nourishing than any that you can buy, but you must not expect it to have exactly the same smooth texture as the commercial kinds.

Ingredients (to serve 5–6)

4 eggs
2 level tablesp. plain flour
2 level teasp. VANILLA
   ESSENCE
¾ teacup caster sugar

1 teacup milk
½–1 teacup cream (according
   to richness desired)

Utensils

2 medium basins
Teacup
Tablespoon
2 freezing trays
Egg whisk

Wooden spoon
Sieve or strainer
DOUBLE SAUCEPAN or bowl
   and saucepan for BAIN-
   MARIE

Time required: About ¾ hr to make, from 1–2 hrs to freeze (according to type of refrigerator).

Method

1. Break eggs and SEPARATE YOLKS FROM WHITES in 2 bowls.
2. Stir sugar into egg yolks with wooden spoon.
3. Sift flour gradually into eggs and sugar, stirring in thoroughly.
4. Stir in milk, very slowly and thoroughly, with wooden spoon, a few drops at a time.
5. Turn into top half of double saucepan (or basin of BAIN-MARIE) and cook over gently boiling water, stir-

ring frequently with wooden spoon, until custard thickens, then carry on stirring for five minutes longer.

6. Remove top half of saucepan and put aside to cool. When no longer steaming, put in refrigerator to chill.

7. Meanwhile, whisk up egg whites until they are so stiff that you can reverse basin without their falling out. (Take care, when you try it!)

8. When custard is quite cold, add vanilla essence and cream, stirring in thoroughly.

9. FOLD egg whites into custard a little at a time, very gently.

10. Fill trays three-quarters full, and freeze quickly, at coldest temperature.

It is not necessary to stir this ice-cream while it is freezing, but if you do stir it (about every 20 mins., until it is half set), you will get a better texture. Leave it alone after this.

Chocolate Ice-cream

Proceed as above as far as 5; then grate about 2 tablesp. plain chocolate, dissolve in about 2 tablesp. hot milk, and add to custard while still warm. Continue as for vanilla ice-cream, but use only ½ teasp. vanilla essence, and reduce amount of cream by about 2 tablesp.

Coffee Ice-cream

Proceed as for vanilla ice-cream as far as 5; then dissolve 1 tablesp. instant coffee in about 2 tablesp. hot milk, and add to custard while still warm. Continue as for vanilla ice-cream, but leave out vanilla essence and reduce amount of cream by about 2 tablesp.

Strawberry, Raspberry, or other Fruit Ices

Proceed as for vanilla ice-cream as far as 7: then replace vanilla essence by 3–4 tablesp. PURÉE of the fruit to be used, stirring in thoroughly when custard is cold. Reduce the amount of cream by 2–3 tablesp. Then continue to end of recipe.

Fruit Salads

A fruit salad can be made from any mixture of fresh fruit in season together with some tinned fruit, or from fresh fruit alone.

If it is to be made from fresh fruit alone, it is best to moisten the fruit with a sugar syrup.

Sugar Syrup (sufficient for 4). Take ½ pt water to 4 oz. sugar; bring to the boil and stir until sugar is dissolved; allow to cool, and add 2 tablesp. lemon or orange juice.

If using the syrup from tinned fruit to moisten the salad, add lemon or orange juice to make fresher flavour.

A good fruit salad should never be mushy, and should offer an element of surprise in flavours and textures. Nuts, particularly BLANCHED and halved almonds or walnuts, are an excellent addition; it is always pleasing to crunch something – and they vastly improve the food value of the salad, as they contain protein, fats, and vitamins. A few dates, cut into four or five pieces, or a handful of sultanas or raisins, also vary flavour and texture, give sweetness (thus making less sugar necessary), and add to the food value.

Don't cut the fruit too small; but pieces should never be so large that they are awkward to eat with a dessertspoon.

To peel oranges or grapefruit easily, put them for a minute

or two in water that is just off the boil. You can then peel off
skin and pith together quickly and cleanly, and the fruit can
be divided into sections (if large cut into two) and the pips
removed, or sliced with a sharp knife. Bananas should be
added just before serving or else soaked in lemon juice to
prevent their turning brown.

For a party, a few tablesp. of maraschino (a liqueur made
from black cherries) or brandy, or for a milder flavour sherry
or marsala, added to the bowl of fruit salad with the syrup,
gives a touch of luxury. A jug of double cream should accompany it. Fruit salads look best in glass bowls.

Oranges with Sugar

One of the nicest desserts I know; also the quickest and
easiest to prepare.

Simply take the largest, sweetest, and juiciest oranges you
can obtain, put them for a minute or two into water which is
just off the boil, after which you can peel off skin and pith
quickly and cleanly. Slice them across fairly thinly, arrange
the slices in individual dishes or in a large glass dish, sprinkle
with caster sugar, and chill.

If you want to serve them at once, it is better to peel them
without putting them in hot water, otherwise they will be
tepid.

Green Figs

Another delicious fruit dish (though expensive out of season,
unless you have a fig tree in your garden) is made by cutting
green figs in halves (the kind we usually get in this country
are not green in fact, but blackish purple and are called so to
distinguish them from dried figs), and sprinkling them with
orange and lemon juice mixed – rather more orange than
lemon. Serve in individual dishes, preferably glass.

Pastry-making without Tears

Pastry-making, more than any other form of cooking, is often surrounded by an aura of phoney mysticism, probably built up by those who are good at it in order to impress those who haven't dared to try. In fact, anyone can learn to make good pastry, though some (like those gardeners known to have green fingers) seem to have a special gift.

There are a number of different ways of making pastry, and different people have their favourite methods; but once you have mastered a method which gives good results, it is as well to stick to it (even though you may have to endure raised eyebrows and remarks such as: 'Oh, I *never* do that!'). By this, I do not mean that you should be afraid to experiment, but simply that some people are more successful with one method than with another.

You will find in this section of the book recipes for *short crust, biscuit crust* (which is a variation of short crust), and a simple *rough puff pastry*. There are other kinds – *suet crust, flaky pastry*, and variations; but when you have mastered the three, you will be able to make successfully, pies, tarts, flans, VOL-AU-VENTS, jam puffs, and many other kinds of savoury or sweet pastry. *Choux pastry* is described under 'Cakes and Pastries'.

An important principle of pastry-making is to keep everything as cold as possible. When the pastry is put into a hot oven, the cold air expands and makes the pastry 'light'. Cool hands are a help; rinse them in cold water before you start. The surface on which you roll your pastry should also be as cold as possible. If you can ever get hold of a marble slab (perhaps off an old washstand), it is the ideal pastry 'board'. Formica table-tops, which most of us have in our kitchens today, do very well; and a wooden board will do too. Work in the coolest spot you can. In summer weather, open doors and windows.

When cutting pastry to fit a plate or dish, never stretch it. If it is not quite the right size or shape, better to 'patch' it with a small piece, moistened underneath with cold water to stick it in place, than stretch it. If you do stretch pastry, it will shrink in cooking and spoil the appearance of the finished article.

Always bake pastry in a hot oven; generally speaking, the richer the pastry (i.e. the more fat there is in it) the hotter the oven. Short pastry has half fat to flour, less than most other kinds, which have two-thirds fat to flour, or more. Arrange oven shelves in correct position before starting.

Short Pastry

Ingredients

(To make 8 oz., sufficient for 1 large – 7 to 7½ in. – flan and 1 smaller, *or* 1

8 oz. plain flour
2 oz. butter or margarine
2 oz. lard

large flan and 3 tartlets,　　Pinch of salt
or 9 to 12 tartlets)　　Approx. 2 tablesp. cold water

Utensils

Rolling-pin　　Sharp knife
Mixing bowl　　Sieve or strainer

Time required: To make, about $\frac{1}{4}$ hr (or a little more). To bake, according to what you are going to use it for – pies and flans, 30–40 mins. or tartlets 20–25 mins.

Method

1. Sift flour and salt into bowl.
2. Cut fat into small pieces and RUB into flour, using fingertips only, until mixture resembles fine bread-crumbs.
3. Mix to stiff dough with water, adding a little at a time and mixing with knife, until all crumbs adhere together. Some flours absorb more water than others, but too much water makes the pastry tough. You may need less than 2 tablesp., but try not to use more.

"FLUTING" A PIE
USE FOREFINGER AND
<u>BACK</u> OF KNIFE

"LEAVES" MADE FROM STRIP OF PASTRY

4. Form dough into a ball with your fingertips. Handle lightly and as little as possible.
5. Roll out lightly on a lightly floured surface with quick, light strokes (*light*, as you see, is the key word) away from you, never towards you. Roll to the thickness you require, then put on a lightly floured dish or plate in the coolest place you can find (a refrigerator if you have one) for $\frac{1}{4}$–$\frac{1}{2}$ hr. Then use as required. Bake in a Fairly Hot oven, Mark 6, 400° F.

When you have to re-roll the pastry for a second cutting, pile all the pieces on top of each other and roll again as before. Use a little flour on the rolling-pin to prevent sticking, but never sprinkle a lot of flour on the pastry.

Biscuit Crust

This is the best kind of short crust to use for fruit or jam tarts or flans. For savoury flans, simply omit sugar.

Ingredients

8 oz. plain flour
5 oz. fat (half butter and half margarine *or* half lard and half butter or margarine)
Pinch of salt
1 level tablesp. caster sugar
1 tablesp. cold water
1 egg yolk

Utensils

Mixing bowl
Small basin
Knife
Sieve or strainer
Rolling-pin
2 cups

Time required: To make, about $\frac{1}{4}$ hr. To bake, as for short pastry.

Method

1. Sift flour and salt into bowl.

2. Cut fat into small pieces and RUB into flour, using fingertips only, until mixture resembles fine bread-crumbs.
3. Put sugar and water in small basin and stir until sugar is dissolved.
4. Break egg and SEPARATE YOLK FROM WHITE in 2 cups. Put white aside for other use (glazing pies or biscuits, making meringue, etc.). Beat yolk into sugar and water.
5. Stir egg-and-sugar mixture into flour and fat mixture, using knife.
6. Form pastry into a ball with fingertips and roll out quickly and lightly on lightly-floured surface. Use as required and bake in Fairly Hot oven, Mark 6, 400° F.

Rough Puff Pastry
(for Sausage Rolls, Jam Puffs, VOL-AU-VENTS, Pies, etc.)

Ingredients

5–6 oz. fat (half butter, half margarine *or* you may use a good cooking fat *or* half lard and half butter or margarine)	8 oz. plain flour Squeeze of lemon juice 6–8 tablesp. cold water

Utensils

Mixing bowl	Knife
Sieve or strainer	Wooden spoon

Time required: To make, about 2 hrs including 'rests'. To bake: sausage rolls and other small things 20–25 mins., pies, etc., about $\frac{1}{2}$ hr if contents are cooked, or according to individual recipes.

Method

1. Sift flour and salt into basin.
2. Cut butter and margarine into pieces about the size of a small walnut, dropping them into the flour as you cut

and stirring round with knife to coat each piece with
flour.

3. Add lemon juice, just a few drops. This makes the dough
more elastic. Then mix to stiff dough with very cold
water, using wooden spoon so as not to break up pieces
of fat; 6–8 tablesp. will be required, much more than
for short pastry. Add water a few drops at a time, until
there is no more loose flour.

4. Gather up dough with fingertips and KNEAD just enough
to bind together. Then roll out on lightly floured surface
as nearly as possible to a rectangle about three times as
long as it is wide.

5. Divide pastry into three with your eye; then fold in three
by folding the end nearest you upwards and the other
end down towards you and over the rest, like an en-
velope.

6. Turn pastry round so that folded edge is to your left.
Lightly press the three open edges with rolling pin to seal
them; then press two or three times across pastry to trap
the air. (This is what makes pastry puff up.)

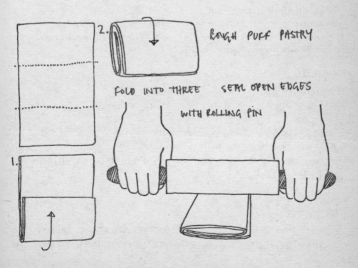

ROUGH PUFF PASTRY

FOLD INTO THREE   SEAL OPEN EDGES
WITH ROLLING PIN

7. Put pastry on lightly floured plate or dish in refrigerator or cool larder, to 'rest' for about 15 mins. Then roll out again to the same approximate size, and fold and press again exactly as before. Use the lightest possible touch. Keep folded edge always on same side.
8. Repeat this process three more times – five rollings in all – 'resting' the pastry after each rolling. Give it a final rest of at least 20 mins. before using; but it is preferable to put it away in the refrigerator or larder until the following day.

The pastry may be kept in the refrigerator in a plastic bag or wrapped in foil for a week or more, if required.

Cakes and Pastries

Health and vitality, complexion, figures, teeth, hair – all would be vastly improved if we ate fewer cakes, pastries, and puddings and more cheese, fruit, and fresh vegetables.

Generally speaking, we in England eat far too much sugar. Eat cakes and pastries by all means, but few and good. Try to make a rule that you only eat what is made at home, and don't break it too often. There is really no sacrifice involved, for most British bakers and confectioners seem to make cakes which, while as crudely and brightly coloured as possible, actually taste of nothing at all. Let me hasten to exclude our fruit cakes and biscuits, both of which are eagerly and deservedly sought after abroad – but pastries are not our strong point, as you will know if you have eaten them in France, Austria or Switzerland.

The recipes in this section are all simple enough to do. Some are for 'everyday' cakes, though if you value your figures, it would be inadvisable to eat them every day; others are intended for 'occasions'.

When using artificial colourings in cooking cakes (or anything else), always use them very sparingly indeed. The object is to make the food more appetizing, not just more noticeable.

Coconut Fingers

Ingredients (to make about 1 doz.)

2 oz. butter *or* margarine	5 oz. desiccated coconut
3 oz. sugar	Pinch of salt
2 oz. self-raising flour	Butter for greasing
2 eggs	

Utensils

2 medium basins	Greaseproof paper
Wooden spoon	Pastry-brush
Sieve or strainer	Small saucepan
Shallow rectangular baking tin	PALETTE KNIFE
Wire tray	Skewer
Cup	Scissors

Time required: 30–40 mins.

Method

1. Set oven to Moderate, Mark 5, 380° F.
2. Melt a little butter in small saucepan, and grease tin well with pastry-brush. Cut greaseproof paper to fit base of tin, press it in, and brush paper over with melted butter. Make sure sides of tin are very well greased.
3. Warm basin for a minute at bottom of oven. CREAM butter and sugar.
4. Break one egg into cup, and add to creamed mixture, beating in thoroughly with wooden spoon. Add second

egg when first is well incorporated (breaking into cup first to check that it is fresh).
5. Add 4 oz. desiccated coconut. Mix well.
6. Sieve flour and salt into basin. Add to mixture, a little at a time, mixing in well.
7. Turn mixture into prepared tin, smooth with PALETTE KNIFE, and bake on second shelf from top of oven for about 20 mins. Test by plunging skewer into cake; if it comes out clean, cake is done.
8. Remove from oven and allow to cool for 2 or 3 mins. Then turn out on to wire tray and leave until quite cold.
9. Ice the cake (see below), and cut into fingers.

Glacé or Water Icing

Ingredients

8 oz. icing sugar
About 1 tablesp. water and
  1 tablesp. lemon juice *or*
  2 tablesp. water

Colouring if wished

Utensils

Sieve
2 medium basins
Tablespoon

Skewer
Large plate, or sheet of paper
Palette knife

Method

1. Sieve icing sugar into basin.
2. Add the water (hot) and lemon juice, a few drops at a time, stirring well until the icing will coat the back of the spoon without running off too fast.
3. Dip skewer into bottle of colour and allow a drop at a time to fall into sugar, stirring continuously until desired colour is produced. Remember that you want a delicate pink or green; a very little colouring goes a long way.
4. Have a basin or saucepan of almost boiling water to hand.

5. Stand cake on large plate or sheet of clean paper, and pour icing over centre, letting it run over as much of the cake as it will cover unaided. Smooth and tidy the edges with the palette knife dipped into hot water.

While icing is still tacky, sprinkle cake with remaining desiccated coconut. When quite set, cut cake into as many fingers as required.

Gingerbread

Ingredients

2 oz. butter
8 oz. golden syrup
  To weigh this, sprinkle the scales well with flour and the syrup will then slide off easily: 1 level tablesp. syrup weighs about 2 oz. (sprinkle spoon with flour first)
1 oz. brown sugar (Barbados if you can get it)
8 oz. plain flour

1 egg
1 level teasp. bicarbonate of soda
1 gill ($\frac{1}{4}$ pt) milk
2 level dessertsp. ground ginger
1 level dessertsp. mixed spice
1 or 2 oz. WHOLE PEEL (optional)
Butter or lard for greasing

Utensils

Medium saucepan
Small saucepan
Mixing bowl
Small basin
Shallow rectangular baking tin (about 5 or 6 in. by 9 in.)
Skewer

Wire tray
Fork
Wooden spoon
Greaseproof paper
Scissors
Pastry-brush
Sieve or strainer

Time required: About 1 hr

Method

1. Set oven to Moderate, Mark 4, 355° F.

2. Melt a little butter or lard in small saucepan and paint inside of tin with pastry-brush. Cut greaseproof paper to fit bottom of tin and four pieces to fit sides and line tin (see Lining a Cake Tin, p. 155). Paint greaseproof paper with melted butter or lard.

3. Put butter, sugar, and syrup in saucepan and melt over gentle heat. Do not allow to boil.

4. Sift flour, bicarbonate, spice, and ginger together into mixing bowl.

5. Break egg in small basin, add milk, and beat well.

6. Pour melted butter, sugar, and syrup into bowl containing dry ingredients, and mix well with wooden spoon.

7. Add egg and milk. Beat well. Add PEEL if using and mix again.

8. Turn into lined tin and bake on middle shelf of oven for about 40 mins. Test by inserting skewer into centre of cake. If it comes out clean, cake is done.

9. Turn on to wire tray and allow to cool before cutting into squares.

Sultana Sponge Cakes

If you learn this phrase: 'The weight of the eggs in sugar, in fat, and in flour', you have a basic sponge mixture fixed in your memory which you may use just as it is, or with the addition of dried fruit, cocoa, jam, a sweet sauce, icing, as cake or pudding, hot or cold. It turns up trumps every time.

Ingredients (to make 12–15 cakes)

2 eggs (the average weight of an egg is 2 oz.)
The weight of the eggs in:
    Granulated sugar
    Butter or margarine
    Self-raising flour
Vanilla essence
2 oz. sultanas
Salt
2 level teasp. caster sugar

Utensils

2 fairly large basins
Wooden spoon
12–15 paper bun-cases and
  a baking tray, or bun-tins
  for 12–15 cakes

Strainer or sieve
Clean cloth
Wire tray
Teaspoon
Pointed knife

Time required: About 15 mins. to make, 15–20 mins. to cook.

Method

1. Set the oven to Fairly Hot, Mark 6, 400° F. (Adjustable shelves should be at second from top and second from bottom, if you need both.)

2. Set paper cases, which are ready for use, on a baking tray; or grease bun-tins well with butter and sprinkle them with a mixture of 1 teasp. flour, 1 teasp. caster sugar. This is best done by putting a little in each and shaking the tin from side to side (over the sink). It prevents the sultanas from sticking to the tins. Tap on bottom to remove surplus.

3. Put sultanas in strainer and wash thoroughly under running water, turning them with your fingers. Shake off surplus water and turn sultanas on to clean cloth. Pat and press dry, and leave temporarily rolled in dry cloth.

4. Warm basin for a minute at bottom of oven. Put in sugar and butter (or margarine) and CREAM them well.

5. Break in one egg and beat it in thoroughly with wooden spoon. Repeat with other egg. Beat until mixture is light and creamy and sugar almost dissolved.

6. Put a pinch of salt in the flour. Dry strainer thoroughly and sift flour and salt into second bowl.

7. Add flour and salt to mixture, a little at a time, FOLD-ING it in lightly. If the mixture is at all stiff – it should be soft and creamy and drop easily from the spoon – add a few drops of cold water.

8. Add 3 or 4 drops VANILLA ESSENCE. Mix in well.

9. Add sultanas, and stir in well.

10. Fill paper cases or bun tins – not much more than half full.
11. Bake for 15–20 mins. To see if they are done, press on one with your finger. It should spring back if it is cooked. A safer method is to insert a skewer at the deepest part: if it comes out dry and clean, the cakes are done.
12. Remove from oven and if in paper cases stand them on wire tray to cool. If bun-tins are used, wait two minutes for cakes to shrink from sides of tins, then ease them gently out with a pointed knife and cool on wire tray.

Scones

If someone calls around tea-time and you're out of cake, it takes half an hour to make and bake these scones. Plain, with butter, they're good; with sultanas they have more appeal for a sweet tooth; with jam and cream (clotted for preference, but whipped will do) they're perfect.

Ingredients (to make about 15 small or 10 medium scones)

½ lb. plain flour
2 level teasp. cream of tartar
1 level teasp. bicarbonate of soda
1½–2 oz. butter
1 oz. sugar
½ gill milk or a little more (a gill is ¼ pt)
1½–2 oz. sultanas (if using)
A little lard or butter for greasing
Pinch of salt

Utensils

Basin
Knife
Measuring jug
Baking sheet
Pastry-brush
Teaspoon
Rolling-pin
Small or medium pastry-cutter
Sieve or strainer

Time required: ½ hr

Method
1. Set oven to Hot, Mark 7, 425° F.

2. Grease baking sheet well.
3. Mix flour with salt, cream of tartar, bicarb. – sieve into basin.
4. RUB IN butter with fingertips until the mixture is like very fine breadcrumbs.
5. Add sugar. (If you are using sultanas, wash them in sieve, pat dry in clean cloth, and mix them in now.)
6. Stir in milk, a little at a time, with the knife. Mix to a soft but not gluey dough. When you have picked up nearly all the crumbs of flour from the sides of the basin, add the milk very carefully indeed – a few drips too many will spoil the consistency of the dough. (If you do make it too wet, add a little more flour, but your scones will not be so successful.)
7. Make dough into a ball with your fingertips, and roll out very lightly on a floured surface to about $\frac{1}{2}$ in. thick.
8. Cutting as close together as possible, cut out as many scones as you can. To prevent the dough from sticking to the cutter, dip it in a little heap of flour between cuts. Place the scones straight on the greased baking sheet. Gather the pieces together and roll out again, handling as little as possible. Cut as many more as possible. Repeat until all dough is used. (You will have to mould the last one with your fingers and it will come out looking rather odd.)
9. GLAZE the scones with a little milk (or white of egg) and bake on second shelf from top of oven for 10–15 mins.

Split, butter, and eat hot. Or allow to cool, then split and butter. Serve jam and cream at table.

These scones will keep quite fresh for several days in an air-tight tin; but they are best eaten very fresh.

Chocolate Cake

I have tried innumerable recipes for chocolate cake at different times, and this is certainly one of the simplest and

best. A coating of chocolate icing would make it more festive
for a special occasion.

Ingredients

¼ lb. cooking chocolate	3 eggs
¼ lb. butter	a level teasp. baking powder
¼ lb. sugar	Pinch of salt
2½ oz. plain flour	

Utensils

8 in. cake tin	Grater
Mixing bowl	Scissors
1 medium basin	Greaseproof paper
Wooden spoon	Wire tray
1 cup	
Strainer or sieve	

Time required: About 20 mins. to prepare, 1 hr to cook.

Method

1. Set oven to Moderate, Mark 4, 355° F.
2. Grease and LINE cake-tin (see p. 155).
3. Grate chocolate into mixing bowl and place in oven
   for 2 or 3 mins. to soften chocolate.
4. Mix flour, baking powder, and salt, and sift into small
   basin. If you are using a sieve, turn it deep-side up and
   help the flour through with wooden spoon – using a basin
   a little wider than the sieve.
5. Take bowl from oven, add butter and sugar to chocolate,
   and CREAM them together thoroughly.
6. Break eggs one at a time into cup to check that they are
   fresh; then add to other ingredients, beating each well
   in before adding the next. Beat with wooden spoon till
   mixture is smooth and creamy.
7. Add flour, baking powder, and salt, a little at a time, and
   mix until all ingredients are thoroughly blended.
8. Turn mixture into lined cake-tin, smoothing level with
   spoon.

9. Bake for 1 hr on middle shelf of oven. TEST WITH
SKEWER. Remove from oven and reverse on to wire
tray. Leave to cool for a few minutes, then gently withdraw tin. Remove paper, and by easing it gently on to
palm of your hand for a moment, turn cake right way
up and leave to cool on wire tray.

(A plastic scraper, which can be bought for a few pence, is a
wonderful aid in cake making, enabling you to scrape every
scrap from the basins. Young members of the family accus-
tomed to being called on ' to scrape the bowl', may of course
object.)

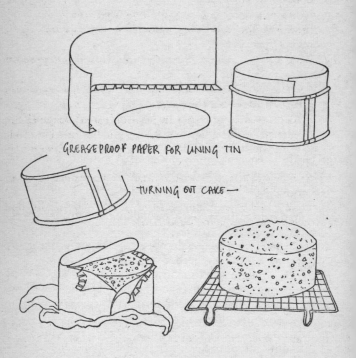

GREASEPROOF PAPER FOR LINING TIN

TURNING OUT CAKE—

Lining a Cake-tin

Greaseproof paper or cooking
  foil
Scissors

Small saucepan
Pastry-brush
A little butter or lard

Method

1. Stand tin on sheet of greaseproof paper or foil, run point
   of scissors round to mark size, remove tin, and cut circle
   of paper to fit bottom.
2. Now cut a strip long enough to go right round tin (with
   small overlap) and deep enough to come about $1\frac{1}{2}$ in.
   higher than tin.
3. Bend up $\frac{1}{2}$ in. along this strip, and snip it with scissors
   about every $\frac{1}{2}$ in.
4. Melt a little fat in saucepan and, using pastry-brush,
   grease inside of tin thoroughly.
5. Place long strip of paper in position round inside of tin,
   so that snipped section lies flat on the bottom. Fit circle
   of paper on top of this. The tin should now be completely
   lined.
6. Paint inside of paper with melted fat, being sure to cover
   completely.

NOTE: It is not always necessary to grease if using foil but
it would be advisable for a fruit cake.

Fruit Loaf

This is splendid for family tea, and for picnics or other
packed meals. It can be cut and eaten as a cake, or sliced
thinly and buttered. You need a bread-tin to bake it in.

Ingredients

$\frac{3}{4}$ lb. plain flour

$\frac{1}{4}$ lb. sugar

¼ lb. butter or margarine
¼ lb. sultanas
¼ lb. currants
1 oz. mixed peel or walnuts
  or both (optional)

1 level teasp. bicarbonate of
  soda
½ an egg
¼ pt milk
A little butter for greasing

Utensils

1 large basin
1 small basin
2 cups
Chopping knife and board
Teaspoon
Pastry-brush

Measuring jug
1 or 2 clean cloths
Strainer or sieve
Small saucepan
Bread tin
Wire tray

Time required: About 1½ hrs

Method

1. Wash sultanas and currants well. (A good way to do this is to put the fruit in a large strainer and run it under warm water, turning it about with your hand for a few moments. Drain and shake off as much water as possible, then dry first in one cloth, then in another. Fruit for a cake must be really dry.)
2. Set oven to Moderate, Mark 5, 380° F.
3. Melt a little butter in small saucepan, and paint it all over inside of tin with pastry-brush. (If this is thoroughly done, there will be no need to line the tin, though a piece of greaseproof or cooking foil cut to fit the bottom of the tin and greased would be an added insurance against burning.)
4. Chop nuts coarsely, if using. If using WHOLE PEEL, chop this coarsely too.
5. RUB FAT INTO FLOUR in large basin.
6. Beat egg lightly in cup. Put half aside in second cup.
7. Put bicarbonate in small basin with milk, and stir till dissolved.
8. Add sugar, beaten egg, and nuts or PEEL or both to flour and fat; add milk with bicarbonate and mix to fairly soft cake mixture.

9. Put mixture in tin, smooth level, and bake for 10 mins. at Mark 5 (380° F.). Then reduce heat to Mark 2 (310° F.) and bake about 2 hrs or until done. Test by plunging a skewer or knife into centre of cake. If it comes out clean and dry, cake is done.

Orange Butterflies

Charming little cakes for tea – especially appreciated at parties for small children.

Ingredients (to make 1 doz.)

2 eggs
The weight of the eggs in:
  Sugar
  Butter or margarine
  Self-raising flour
1 small orange

Butter for greasing
Orange butter icing for filling
  (see p. 158)
Small piece of angelica
  (optional)

Utensils

Tray of 12 patty-pans
Mixing bowl
Medium basin
Wooden spoon
Dessertspoon
Knife

Sieve or strainer
Teaspoon
Grater
Plate
Lemon-squeezer
Wire tray

Time required: 30–40 mins.

Method

1. Set oven to Fairly Hot, Mark 6, 400° F.
2. Grease patty-pans.
3. Weigh eggs, then sugar and butter.
4. Warm mixing bowl in oven. CREAM sugar and butter.
5. Weigh flour and sift into medium basin.
6. Wash orange, dry and grate rind on to plate (1 level

teasp. will be enough). Avoid grating the pith. Squeeze juice from half the orange.

7. Beat eggs into butter and sugar, one at a time, making sure one is well incorporated before adding next.

8. Add orange rind to flour and FOLD this gently into mixture in bowl, a little at a time, together with 1 dessertsp. orange juice. Stir all together gently but thoroughly until thick, creamy mixture results.

9. Half-fill patty-pans. Bake for 15–20 mins. on second shelf from top of oven. When done, allow to cool in pans for a few minutes, then turn out carefully on to wire tray with the aid of a knife and leave to get cold, right side up.

10. Slice off the top from each cake and cut this slice in two. Put a blob of orange butter icing on each cake and re-place the 'wings' to give the effect of a butterfly. If you like, you can imitate the body or the antennae with fine strips of angelica.

If you are short of time whipped cream may be used instead of orange butter icing.

Orange Butter Icing

Ingredients

2 oz. unsalted butter
4 oz. icing sugar
1 level teasp. grated orange rind

1 teasp. orange juice

Utensils

Medium basin
Sieve or strainer
Wooden spoon

Grater
Plate
Lemon-squeezer

Time required: About 10 mins.

Method

1. Sieve icing sugar.
2. CREAM sugar and butter.
3. Grate orange rind. Squeeze juice. Add both to mixture, beating in well.

Cinnamon Butter Biscuits

Some call them Butter Cakes. They are really a cross between the two – crisp and nutty, more substantial than a biscuit, harder textured than a cake.

Ingredients (to make 24–26 biscuits)

2 oz. sweet almonds
¾ lb. plain flour
¼ lb. caster sugar
½ lb. butter

2 eggs
2½ teasp. CINNAMON
A little butter or lard for
  greasing

Utensils

Baking sheet(s)
Rolling-pin
Chopping knife and board
2 cups
1 saucer
Mixing bowl

Pastry-brush
PALETTE KNIFE
Circular pastry cutter, about
  2½ in. diameter
Wooden spoon
Fork
Wire tray

Time required: 1 hr

Method

1. BLANCH almonds. (That is, put them in basin, pour boiling water over, and leave to stand two or three minutes. You can then slip them out of their skins between finger and thumb. Some may take a little longer, or the addition of more boiling water.)
2. Chop almonds fairly fine.

3. Turn on oven to Hot, Mark 7, 425° F. Grease baking sheet(s) with butter or lard.

4. RUB butter into flour.

5. Add sugar, CINNAMON, chopped almonds. Mix well.

6. Break eggs into 2 cups, SEPARATING YOLKS FROM WHITES.

7. Add yolks to rest of ingredients, stir well, then KNEAD well until a clean ball of paste results. Roll this out about $\frac{1}{4}$ in. thick on a floured surface.

8. Cut into rounds and place on baking sheet(s), allowing plenty of room for expansion. Re-roll and cut as often as necessary until all pastry is used.

9. Put a little white of egg on saucer. (Cover cup and put rest aside in cool place for use in meringues, or as meringue to top a pie, or for other uses.) Using pastry-brush, GLAZE each biscuit with lightly beaten white of egg.

10. Bake for about 15 mins. on second shelf from top of oven (and second from bottom, if necessary) until slightly risen, expanded, and golden brown in colour. Allow to cool on baking sheet for a few minutes; then lift on to wire tray with PALETTE KNIFE and leave to get cold.

Brandy Snaps

I am not going to pretend that these are very easy to pull off. There is nothing simpler than the making of the mixture, but whether you succeed in producing neat little rolls or curls after they are baked depends entirely on your own speed and dexterity. If you get some professional-looking ones – well done! If the rest look as if they have been sat on, well – they're all edible, and they're fun to try.

Ingredients (to make about 1 doz. Don't try to make more at one time; or if you must, complete one batch before putting the second in the oven)

2 oz. flour
2 oz. butter
2 oz. sugar, preferably brown
2 oz. syrup or black treacle
  (about 1 level tablesp.)

1 level teasp. ground ginger
Few drops lemon juice
Butter or lard for greasing
Cream for filling

Utensils

Medium saucepan
2 or 3 wooden spoons

Baking sheet

Time required: About ½ hr

Method

1. Set oven to Moderate, Mark 4, 355° F.
2. Grease baking sheet well with butter or lard.
3. Put butter, sugar, and syrup in saucepan and melt gently over low heat. Do not allow to boil.
4. Stir in flour, ginger, and lemon juice.
5. Place small mounds on baking sheet, with as much space between as possible. Bake for about 15 mins. on second shelf from top of oven. Turn off heat.
6. Remove from tin, one at a time, putting baking sheet back in open oven each time you remove one. (If they have run together, cut them apart with a knife.) Curl each snap round the handle of a wooden spoon, remove to a plate, and take the next. Work as fast as possible, as

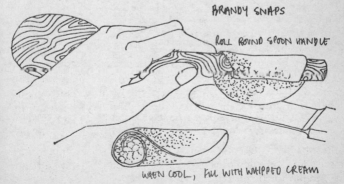

BRANDY SNAPS

ROLL ROUND SPOON HANDLE

WHEN COOL, FILL WITH WHIPPED CREAM

they harden in cooling, and once hard it is impossible to shape them.

When quite cold, fill with whipped cream. This is best done with a teaspoon and one finger.

Meringues

Whenever you have a couple of egg whites going begging (after making MAYONNAISE with the yolks, for instance), you can make delicious meringues with very little trouble. Alternatively you can make meringues when you need them and keep the yolks of the eggs for MAYONNAISE or custards. Allow 2 oz. caster sugar to each egg white.

Ingredients (to make about 8 meringues, or 4 if sandwiched together with cream)

2 egg whites
4 oz. caster sugar

Whipped cream for filling, or
   ice-cream, or both

Utensils

ROTARY BEATER
Medium basin
Tablespoon or dessertspoon,
   or forcing-bag with plain
   nozzle
Baking sheet

Greaseproof paper or cooking
   foil
Pastry-brush
A little salad oil
SPATULA
Teaspoon

Time required: 3 hrs or more

Method

1. Set oven to lowest possible heat.
2. Whisk egg whites stiffly. Add 1 teasp. sugar and whisk again until the whites are so stiff that you can turn the basin upside-down without their falling out. The time this takes depends on the strength of your wrist and the quality of your beater. (Be careful how you do the upside-down test!)

3. FOLD in the rest of the sugar.
4. Grease the baking sheet. Cut greaseproof paper or foil to fit it, lay it on, and paint it with a fine film of oil. This is the best way to ensure getting your meringues off the baking sheet unbroken.
5. Shape the meringues either with large or small spoon (some people use two and dip them into cold water between operations), or pipe them straight on to the greaseproof. You can put them fairly close together, but they must not touch. It doesn't matter if they are a bit irregular in shape, but try to get them about the same size.
6. Bake, or rather, dry in the centre of the oven for about 3 hrs. Leave the oven door just ajar. If it is the kind which opens downwards, put a wooden spoon in to keep it open.
7. When the meringues are dry and crisp and have turned a delicate pinkish gold colour, like clouds at sunset, lift them with SPATULA and remove the soft centre with a teaspoon, or push it gently in. Replace the meringues on their backs and leave another half-hour or so until quite dry.

Keep till quite cold and sandwich together with whipped cream just before serving. Meringues will keep in an airtight tin for a couple of weeks – without the cream, of course.

Chocolate Profiteroles or Éclairs

These delicious little cream buns of *choux* (pronounced 'shoe') pastry look very difficult to make, but they really are not – and they give a very professional air to a party table. Éclairs are made the same way, but the mixture is piped on to the baking sheet in short lengths.

Ingredients (to make 15–20 little buns, or more if you are nimble-fingered enough to make them smaller)

2 oz. plain flour
⅛ pt water
1 oz. butter
Pinch of sugar
Pinch of salt

2 eggs
A few drops of milk
¼ pt double cream and 2
    level teasp. caster sugar
    for filling

Utensils

1 small saucepan
Strainer or sieve
2 medium basins
PALETTE KNIFE
Sharp-pointed knife
Wooden spoon
FORCING-BAG with
    medium-size plain nozzle,
    if possible (alternatively a
    teaspoon)

Sheet of greaseproof or other
    paper
Pastry-brush
Cup
ROTARY BEATER
Fork
Wire rack

Time required: About ½ hr to make and at least ½ hr to cool before filling.

Method

1. Set oven to Fairly Hot, Mark 6, 400° F. Grease baking sheet with butter or lard.
2. Sift flour on to piece of paper.
3. Put butter, water, sugar, and salt in saucepan and heat to boiling point.
4. Beat eggs in basin.
5. Turn down heat, tip in flour all at once, and stir like mad with wooden spoon until mixture forms a clean ball and nothing is left on sides of pan.
6. Now beat in eggs, a little at a time. Remove from heat and beat well until paste is smooth and glossy and will hold its shape. Allow to cool a little.
7. *Either* fill forcing-bag with pastry and pipe tiny rounds on to baking sheet, *or* make little mounds with teaspoon. Do not place them too close together, but bear in mind how many you have to find room for; you may need two baking sheets, or a sponge sandwich tin to help out.
8. Brush each bun with a little milk.

9. Bake on centre shelf of oven about 15 mins. until well risen. Remove from oven, make a small gash in each with sharp, pointed knife, and return to oven for a few mins. to dry. When they are done, there should be no more beads of moisture visible on the surface.
10. Lift on to wire rack with palette knife and allow to cool.
11. Whip cream with 1 teasp. sugar.

To Fill

When buns are quite cold, slice the top *almost* but not quite off each with sharp knife, so that you can raise it like a flap; either use forcing-bag (previously washed free of *choux* pastry, of course) to fill with cream, or simply use a teaspoon. Do not over-fill. Close the flap down again afterwards.

Chocolate Icing

Ingredients

1½ oz. plain chocolate (cooking chocolate may be bought at some confectioner's or at health food stores but any dark chocolate will do)
1 tablesp. water (or a little more, if icing seems too thick)

¼ lb. icing sugar
2 or 3 drops VANILLA ESSENCE
1 or 2 drops glycerine or salad oil (to give a glossy finish)

Utensils

1 small basin
1 medium saucepan

Wooden spoon

Time required: 5–10 mins.

Method

1. Break up chocolate and heat in BAIN-MARIE, with the water, until chocolate is dissolved.

2. Sift sugar and add to chocolate and water. Add VANILLA
   ESSENCE. Stir well until smooth and liquid. Add
   glycerine or salad oil. Stir well.

To ice *profiteroles*, pick each one up with your fingers and dip
the top into the warm icing. Replace on wire tray and allow
to set.

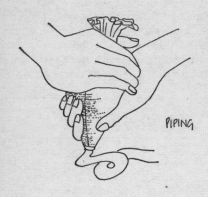

PIPING

Drinks That Don't Come out of a Bottle

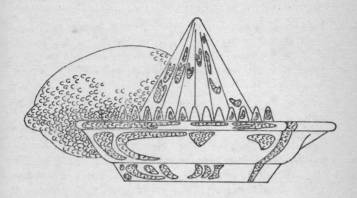

Lemon Squash

This is very much more wholesome, particularly for children and invalids, than the ready-bottled variety.

Ingredients

4 medium size lemons
¼ lb. demerera sugar
9 pts water

Utensils

Sharp knife or potato peeler
Large jug or other receptacle
   (not glass)
Spoon for stirring
Basin
Kettle

Time required: 10–15 mins. plus time for lemon squash to become quite cold

Method

1. Wash and dry the lemons, remove any flaws or printed brand marks with a sharp knife. Peel two of them as thinly as possible, leaving all the pith behind. (A potato peeler makes a good tool for this job.) Put peelings into jug.

2. Boil some water. Put the peeled lemons in basin, pour boiling water over them, leave for about a minute. Remove first one, then the other, run them for a moment under the cold tap. You can then peel all the pith cleanly away from the flesh with ease.

3. Repeat with the unpeeled lemons, this time discarding all or most of the peelings. Too much peel in the squash tends to make it bitter. (The lemons should not be left to soak in the hot water for more than a minute or so – no matter how much squash you are making – or juice and flavour will be extracted and wasted. Put a few in the water at a time, and top up from a boiling kettle if necessary.)

4. Slice the lemons, now pared down to the flesh, thinly across, cut slices into four and remove all pips. Add lemon flesh to peel.

5. Add the sugar.

6. Bring the 3 pts water to the boil and pour it over the fruit and sugar. Stir, cover, and leave to get quite cold. Serve iced if possible.

Orange squash can be made in the same way, using a little less sugar.

Lemonade
(for dilution with water as required)

Ingredients (to make about 3½ pts)

6 good-sized lemons	1 oz. tartaric acid

4½ lb. granulated sugar

3 pts water

2 level teasp. Epsom salts

2 oz. citric acid
(these produce the fizz)

Utensils

Grater

Lemon-squeezer

2 large bowls

Spoon

Sieve or fine strainer

Jug

Bottles to hold about 3½ pts,
with corks or screw tops

Time required: About ½ hr

Method

NOTE: Avoid enamel utensils. There is sometimes a chemical reaction.

1. Wash bottles thoroughly in very hot water and a little detergent. Rinse very well.

2. Wash lemons and grate rind finely into bowl.

3. Squeeze juice and add, with sugar, acids, and Epsom salts.

4. Bring water to boil and pour over other ingredients. Stir well. Allow to stand till next day.

5. Pour through fine sieve into second bowl.

6. Using jug alone, or jug and funnel, fill bottles and close with corks or screw tops.

Iced Tea

Very cold, clear tea with lemon is one of the most refreshing drinks imaginable in hot weather.

Ingredients (to make just over 3 pts)

1 quart of strong tea

2 lemons

1 pt water

About 2 tablesp. sugar (less
or more according to
taste)

Utensils

Teapot   Lemon-squeezer
Large jug   Strainer
Large glass jug   Tablespoon

Time required: about 10 mins. (plus time to get cold)

Method

1. Make tea in usual way and strain into jug.
2. Cut two thin slices from one lemon. Squeeze juice from the rest and from other lemon. Add to tea.
3. Add 1 pt water. Add sugar, 1 tablesp. at a time, tasting carefully before you add more. The tea should not be too sweet.
4. Chill thoroughly, and serve in glass jug with lemon slices floating on top.

Spiced Cider
(hot or cold)

Ingredients (to serve 10)

2 quarts dry cider   1 lemon
1 rounded teasp. ALLSPICE   1 orange
   (whole)   1 tablesp. demerara sugar
6 cloves   (or more, to taste)
1 STICK OF CINNAMON

Utensils

Large saucepan   Cotton thread or fine string
Tablespoon   Lemon-squeezer
Square of muslin or fine cotton

Method

1. Put spices in muslin, gather up corners, and tie with cotton thread into small bag. If necessary, break the CINNAMON stick in two to make this easier.

2. Put bag of spices in saucepan and pour on cider. Bring to boil and SIMMER gently for $\frac{1}{4}$ hr.
3. Squeeze lemon and orange.
4. After $\frac{1}{4}$ hr remove bag of spices and add lemon and orange juice. Stir well, taste, and add sugar as required. Don't make it too sweet.
5. Reheat and serve at once, remembering to put a spoon into each glass before you pour in the scalding liquid – unless you want a series of cracked glasses.

Alternatively, leave until quite cold; serve straight from the refrigerator, if you have one.

It looks attractive if you have a very thin slice of lemon or orange in each glass.

Elderflower Champagne

This is a delectable drink made from the flowers of the elder tree, which grows freely in town gardens and prolifically in the countryside. The 'champagne' takes only two weeks to mature.

If you have no elder tree in your garden or street, look around the local car-parks, squares, schools – any odd green corner may produce one of these rather coarse-looking shrubby trees bearing great flat heads of creamy fragrant flowers in summer and clusters of handsome reddish-purple berries in autumn (which can be used to make the much more potent elderberry wine). Make quite sure you have the right tree.

Ingredients (to make 8 pts)

2 large heads of elder flowers, fully opened and, if possible, picked when the sun is on them
1½ lb. sugar

1 lemon
2 tablesp. white WINE VINEGAR
4 quarts (1 gallon) water

T–G

Utensils

A gallon jar or crock of
  earthenware, glass, or
  stoneware (any vessel not
  made of metal and
  sufficiently large would do,
  at a pinch)
Well washed, strong bottles –
  beer, cider, or mineral water
  bottles are best – to contain
  8 pts

Lemon-squeezer
Potato-peeler or sharp knife
Funnel
Tablespoon
Strainer

Time required: To make, ¼ hr; to stand, 24 hrs; to keep, 2 weeks.

Method

1. Wash lemon and peel the rind as thinly as possible (a potato-peeler is the best tool for this, or use a very sharp knife). Wash flower-heads quickly in cold water.
2. Squeeze lemon and put juice in vessel together with rind and flower-heads, just as they are.
3. Add sugar and WINE VINEGAR.
4. Pour on 1 gall. of cold water. Leave to stand 24 hrs.
5. Now strain (with the help of funnel) into bottles, and cork firmly.

The 'champagne' should be effervescent and ready to drink in about 2 weeks.

Claret Cup

This is a good drink to serve at a young people's party or any summer party. Claret is the name given in England for the past six or seven hundred years to the red wines of Bordeaux. The word comes from the French 'clairet', used to distinguish the lighter red wines of the Bordeaux region from the darker wines of more southern vineyards. Red Bordeaux wines are always abundant, consistently good, and some of them very cheap. You can buy a suitable claret for a party in a half-gallon jar, the equivalent of 3 bottles, for about £2.

Ingredients (for 8–10 wine glasses)

2 lemons	¼ pt water
2 oranges	½ syphon soda
1 bottle claret	A few sprigs of mint (or
4 oz. sugar	borage, if you can get it)

Utensils

Lemon-squeezer	Tablespoon
Large jug or bowl	Strainer
Small basin	Funnel

Time required: About ¼ hr, plus time to chill

Method

1. Wash oranges and lemons and remove a few fine strips of rind. (The best way to do this is with a potato-peeler.)
2. Squeeze fruit and strain into jug. Add claret.
3. Put sugar in small basin, pour on ¼ pt warm water and stir till sugar is dissolved. Add this to contents of jug. Add a good sprig of mint (washed). Stir, and chill in refrigerator or leave in coldest place you have for at least 1 hr.
4. Just before serving, add soda water.

Serve with small sprig of mint (or borage), or a tiny strip of lemon or orange rind, in each glass.

Sangria

This is a Spanish summer drink, very similar to Claret Cup but made with the heavier Spanish red wine and sometimes made sickly by the addition of too much sugar.

Ingredients (for 8–10 wine glasses)

1 bottle Spanish red wine

Caster sugar to taste, about
   4 oz.
1 orange
1 lemon

About ⅓ siphon of soda water
A good dash of brandy if
   possible

Utensils

1 large glass jug
Lemon-squeezer

Long spoon to stir

Time required: about ¼ hr, plus time to chill

Method

1. Wash fruit, cut one or two thick slices from each and put these in jug.
2. Squeeze remainder of orange and lemon and add juice to jug.
3. Add sugar.
4. Pour on wine and stir.
5. Add brandy and stir.
6. Taste, and add more sugar if required but the drink should not be too sweet.
7. Chill.
8. Add ice cubes and soda water, and serve.

Coffee

Instant coffee is quite a pleasant drink but it never tastes anything like as good as 'proper' coffee, made from the freshly ground beans in one of the traditional ways.

There are a number of methods of making good coffee, with or without special contraptions – filters, expresso pots, percolators, etc. Points to remember are:

1. Have the coffee as fresh as possible, either ground at home in your own coffee mill, or bought (freshly ground to

the size that suits the kind of coffee-maker you use) in small quantities. And keep it in an airtight jar. Some of the tinned vacuum-sealed coffees are excellent too.

2. Use *enough* coffee. You cannot make good coffee if you are stingy with the quantity. A heaped dessertsp. per cup is about right.

3. However you make it, never allow coffee to boil. Remember that *coffee boiled is coffee spoiled*. Don't let the milk boil either – it ruins the flavour of the coffee. Use the creamiest milk available, and heat plenty. Lots of people like equal quantities of milk and coffee, especially at breakfast-time.

If you have no coffee-making gadgets, the best way to make it is the simplest: in a jug, preferably earthenware.

Method (to serve 4 cups of black coffee or 8 cups of white)

1. Boil a pint of fresh cold water.
2. Heat jug and coffee-pot, or 2 jugs, by filling with very hot water and standing for a minute or two. Pour off water from first jug, shaking out last drops.
3. Put in coffee – 4 heaped dessertsp., medium-ground.
4. Pour on boiling water, and stand for a minute. Then give a good stir with cold metal spoon (this helps to sink the grounds) and stand again in a warm place for about 4 mins.
5. Pour off water from coffee-pot or second jug, shake last drops out, and pour coffee in through very fine strainer.

If white coffee is required, heat an equal quantity of milk (being careful not to let it boil) while the coffee is standing, and serve in separate heated jug. If you like your white coffee strong, less milk will be needed, of course, or you can serve single or double cream.

If you want black, after-dinner coffee, served in the tiny cups known as *demi-tasses*, make the coffee stronger.

Demerara sugar is often preferred though I personally think it spoils the taste of the coffee.

Coffees vary in flavour considerably according to where they grow and how the beans are roasted. The only way to discover your preferences is by frequent experiment.

Iced Coffee

Make black or white coffee as above, sweeten it to taste, and chill. Add cream just before serving. A blob of whipped cream on top gives it an air of luxury. Serve in tall glasses, with straws, if possible.

Caramel Milk Shake

Milk is a splendid food for everyone at any age. If you are underweight or merely consider yourself too thin, drink as much of it as you can. A delicious milk shake, if you don't care for it neat, is made with caramel (see recipe for Crème Caramel, p. 126). It is a good idea to make a pint or so of caramel at a time and keep it in a covered jar or bottle for use with milk puddings, stewed fruit, or milk shakes.

Simply put 1 tablesp. caramel for each tumbler of milk required, into a wide-mouthed jug or a bowl and whisk a little. Serve as cold as possible.

A portion of vanilla ice-cream dropped into each glass gives you a treat for children's elevenses or on a hot evening – Caramel Milk Glacé, if you want to be grand.

Jams and Preserves

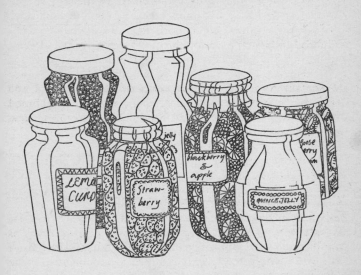

Never let yourself be frightened by tales of the difficulties of making jam. As long as you follow a few simple rules conscientiously, there is absolutely nothing to it. Even strawberry jam, which is notoriously difficult to set, has never failed me when I use the recipe on p. 179.

Jam, like wine, will vary in quality according to the climate of the season. In a good year, when there has been plenty of sun and sufficient rain, jam will be better than in a sunless year or after a season of drought. This aspect of jam-making is beyond your control. All the rest is within it.

As to equipment, you need a preserving-pan or a thick, heavy saucepan. An enamel pan which has suffered the slightest damage will burn and therefore will not do. Don't use a very large vessel to cook a small amount of jam in – it is wasteful. The only other 'tool' you need is a long-handled wooden spoon.

Keep to the quantities in the recipe and remember that jars must be bone-dry and hot and that jam must either be covered at once while hot, or allowed to get quite cold – no half measures. And it must be stored in a cool, dry place.

Some fruits contain much more pectin (a substance essential for a good 'jell') than others, and some lack acid. You can add pectin artificially by buying a patent setting-agent, but it is greatly preferable simply to add a little fruit with a high pectin content, not enough noticeably to alter the flavour of the jam but sufficient to set it – red currants or gooseberries are customarily used. Acid may be added in the form of citric or tartaric acid, obtainable from chemist or grocer; or sometimes lemon juice is used.

It is more economical to make jam in large batches than in small ones.

When buying soft fruit for jam there is invariably some wastage. Strawberries sold commercially as 'jam strawberries' are cheaper but often contain a high proportion of soft or damaged ones which must be cut or thrown out: you cannot make good jam with poor fruit. Add to this the weight of the hulls, and you will need to buy an extra pound to every five you require if you are to have a safe margin. If the fruit is home-grown or fresh-picked, the margin will be much slighter.

Potting Jam

Take the greatest possible care to arrange everything comfortably within your reach, so that no accident can occur. Boiling jam spilt on the skin will cause horrible scalds. Allow one or two extra jars. You might get an unexpectedly quick set, hence slightly more jam – or you might break a jar.

When jam has reached setting point, put your pre-heated jars ready standing on thick newspaper and preferably on a strong tray. Have ready a well-washed and dried jug with a good pouring spout. Take one jar at a time, stand it apart

from the others (to avoid dripping jam all over the other jars),
and fill from the jug. When the preserving-pan is nearly
empty, and if it has a lip, you should be able to pour straight
from the pan into the jars. I find it helpful to wear clean
rubber gloves throughout this operation.

Testing for a set

Put a little jam on a saucer and stand it in a cool place for a
few minutes. Then tip the saucer, or push your finger along
the surface of the jam. If a set has been reached, wrinkles will
form.

Strawberry Jam

Ingredients (to make 13–14 lb.)

8 lb. strawberries (after
  HULLING and picking
  over)

1 lb. gooseberries
$\frac{1}{2}$ oz. tartaric or citric acid
7$\frac{1}{2}$ lb. granulated sugar

Utensils

Sufficient jars to contain up
  to 15 lb. jam
Packet of jam covers
Preserving-pan or large thick
  saucepan
Long-handled wooden spoon
Long-handled spoon for
  skimming

Large colander
2 large bowls for washing
  fruit (saucepans would do)
Knife
Saucer
Scissors
Large dish or dishes to hold
  sugar

Time required: Variable (according to your speed in preparing fruit, washing jars, and other factors); you had better
allow yourself an entire morning or afternoon – certainly a
couple of hours.

Method

1. Top and tail gooseberries with scissors, wash in colander, and put in preserving-pan.
2. Wash strawberries thus: fill large bowl with cold water and gently immerse fruit. Strain it off into colander in batches, putting clean fruit in second bowl. If the berries are very dirty you may need to repeat this process, but handle them as gently as possible in order not to bruise them and lose juice.
3. When fruit is reasonably clean, hull it, and weigh exact quantities required. Then put it in pan with gooseberries.
4. Add acid, and cook gently on low heat, stirring frequently, until fruit is soft, about ½ hr.
5. Meanwhile, wash jars thoroughly in hot water, drain, and place in oven upside-down or on sides. Turn oven on at Very Slow, Mark 1, 290° F.
6. Weigh out sugar, put in large dish or dishes, and place in oven to warm.
7. When fruit is soft, add sugar all at once, and stir until it has dissolved and no longer feels gritty. Bring to the boil fairly fast. Watch that jam does not boil over.
8. Boil fast for about 15 mins. TEST FOR SETTING (p. 179). If a set has been reached, skim off the top layer of scum quickly; stir the rest in and remove jam from heat at once.
9. In the case of strawberry jam, when it is pleasant to have some whole fruit distributed throughout the jam, it is advisable to wait 15 mins. before potting, otherwise the fruit may all rise to the top of the jars. Then pot as described.

Gooseberry Jam

You can make gooseberry jam (one of the easiest jams to set) with just gooseberries, when it tends to be somewhat thick and gluey, or with red or white currants, both of which make a very good jam. A more unusual jam is made with the rind and juice of oranges. This preserve has a delicate flavour and an excellent consistency.

Ingredients (to make about 8–8½ lb. jam)

4 lb. green gooseberries	¾ pt water
4 lb. granulated sugar	2 juicy oranges

Utensils

Packet of jam covers	Measuring jug
Jars to hold up to 10 lb.	Grater
Preserving-pan or large thick saucepan	Lemon-squeezer
	Colander
Scissors	Large dish or dishes to hold sugar
Wooden spoon	

Time required: Variable – allow yourself 2 hrs (the cooking will take approx. ¾ hr)

Method

1. Top and tail gooseberries with scissors and wash in colander.
2. Wash jars in hot water, drain well, and place in oven upside-down or on sides. Turn over on at Very Slow, Mark 1, 290° F.
3. Pour sugar into dish or dishes, and place in oven to warm.
4. Put gooseberries in preserving-pan with water. Heat slowly, breaking the fruit up with wooden spoon as it softens.
5. Wash oranges, grate rind finely into gooseberries. Squeeze juice and add to rest.
6. When fruit is soft, add warm sugar, stir thoroughly until it is dissolved and no longer feels gritty.
7. Bring jam to the boil gradually, then boil rather fast. This jam will set quickly. TEST FOR SETTING after 15 mins.
8. Pot as described at beginning of chapter. Cover at once, or allow to get quite cold before doing so.

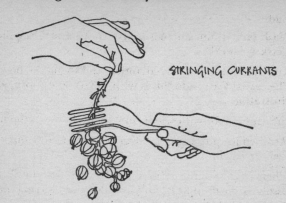

STRINGING CURRANTS

Blackcurrant Jam

This is one of the easiest jams to make successfully. In addition to its excellent flavour, its firm consistency and rich dark colour make it splendid for use in jam tarts. If you like your jam very sweet, you may add a little more sugar than is given in this recipe.

Ingredients (to make 8 lb.)

4 lb. blackcurrants
4 lb. granulated sugar

2 pts water

Utensils

Packet of jam covers
Jars to hold up to 10 lb.
  preserve
Preserving-pan or large, thick
  saucepan
Wooden spoon

Large basin
Large dish or dishes to hold
  sugar
Measuring jug
Fork
Colander

Time required: Variable (STRINGING the fruit is a slow job – try to get a helper); cooking approx. ¾ hr.

Method

1. Wash jars, drain, and set to dry in oven at Very Slow, Mark 1, 290° F.

2. Rinse the fruit, drain in colander, and string the berries. The easiest way to do this is with the back of a fork, as in illustration.

3. Put fruit in pan with water and bring slowly to the boil.

4. Meanwhile, put sugar in dish or dishes, and place in oven to warm.

5. When fruit is quite tender, add sugar, stir until it is dissolved, turn up heat, and boil jam fast, stirring often. TEST FOR SETTING after about 15 mins.

6. Pot as described at beginning of chapter. Cover at once, or allow to get quite cold first.

Plum Jam

This can be the most insipid of all jams, but the following recipe (best made with the small black plums which begin the plum season) makes a spicy preserve, not as tart as damson jam but with an agreeable bite to it.

Ingredients (to make 6–7 lb.)

5 lb. dark plums	5 CLOVES
3 lb. sugar	1 teasp. tartaric acid

Utensils

Packet of jam covers	Strainer
Jars to hold up to 8 lb.	Sharp knife
Preserving-pan	Teaspoon
Wooden spoon	Large china, glass, or plastic
Perforated spoon	bowl
	Light hammer

Time required: This recipe requires the fruit to stand for 24 hrs; preparation time is variable, depending on ripeness of plums, and cooking time about 45 mins.

Method

1. Wash fruit, cut in halves, and remove as many stones as will part easily from the flesh. Keep a couple of dozen stones. Sometimes hardly any will come away. Don't worry, they will rise to the surface during cooking and can be skimmed off. Put fruit in bowl.
2. Pour sugar over and leave for 24 hrs.
3. Next day, wash jars in hot water, drain, and set to dry in oven at Very Slow, Mark 1, 290° F.
4. Put fruit, with syrup which will have formed, and any undissolved sugar, into preserving-pan. Add CLOVES and tartaric acid. Bring slowly to boil and SIMMER until fruit is tender, stirring often.
5. Skim off stones with perforated spoon as they rise, and collect them in strainer. When you have got them all out, rub them around strainer with wooden spoon to obtain any pulp still clinging to them; scrape it from underside of strainer and add to jam.
6. Crack the stones you have kept on a hard surface (*not* a formica table-top) with the hammer. Add the almondy kernels to the jam just before it has finished cooking. (This is optional.)
7. Stir the scum in, until the jam is cooked; then thinly skim off any that remains on the surface. TEST FOR SETTING after 15 mins. The jam sets quickly – don't overcook.
8. Pot (see p. 178) and cover at once, or leave until quite cold to cover.

Quince Jelly

Small quantities of quinces, looking like highly decorative golden pears and with a strong, sweet smell, come into the shops in late autumn, especially in country districts: look out for them. They make a jelly which some people will almost sell their souls for. It is beautiful to look at – a rich pinkish-amber colour, and excellent to eat with pork or duck, as well as on bread and butter.

Exact quantities and time cannot be given for this recipe. Start off with your quinces, a lot or a few, and the rest will follow naturally.

Ingredients

Quinces
Sugar (1 lb. to each pt of quince juice)

Water (about 1 pt to each lb. of quinces)

Utensils

A packet of jam covers
A number of small jars
Preserving-pan
Thick saucepan
Wooden spoon

Large square of fine muslin for jelly-bag
Piece of string
Large basin

Time required: Variable – preparing and cooking about 2 hrs, straining several hours, reboiling ¾ hr.

Method

1. Peel quinces and cut into thick slices without removing cores. Put them in preserving-pan with just sufficient water to float them. Bring to the boil and cook gently until quite tender – about 1½ hrs or longer. Mash the fruit down with wooden spoon as it cooks, until all is reduced to a pulp.

2. Place the square of muslin in the basin with the edges hanging over the sides. Now turn the fruit into the centre of the muslin, gather up the four corners so that you have a bag, and tie it tightly, leaving a long loop of string with which to hang the bag.

3. Hang the bag on a hook or nail in such a position that you can place the basin underneath to catch the juice.

Leave it to drip for several hours (overnight if you like) until no more juice is dripping in the basin. *Do not press or squeeze the bag, or the jelly will not be clear.*

4. Wash jars, drain, and set to dry in oven at Very Slow, Mark 1, 290° F.

5. Measure the amount of juice carefully and *allow 1 lb. of sugar to each pot of juice.*

6. Put juice and sugar into pan. (If there is not much, choose a small pan; an ordinary saucepan will do, provided it is thick and will not burn.) Bring to boil and boil about ¾ hr. Then TEST FOR SETTING.

7. Pot into small jars and cover at once or when quite cold.

If you cannot find a suitable place to hang your bag, try using an upturned chair.

Pear Preserve

Old gardens often contain a tree which bears great masses of large, coarse, brownish pears of indeterminate species which have the texture of carrots but not as much taste, and hardly seem worth the trouble of picking. In autumn you find a few baskets of them in small greengrocers' shops labelled 'Fine for Stewing', which indeed they are; and they store well, too. But if you would like to have a constant supply of a really luscious sweet which you would be proud to offer to guests at a dinner party, try the following recipe. Any cooking pears may be used.

Ingredients

6 lb. pears after peeling and
  coring (start with 7–8 lb.)
2 lb. sugar, preferably
  demerara

½ pt vinegar
½ pt water

Utensils

Preserving-pan or large, thick
  saucepan
Knife

Large stoneware or glass jar
  or jars
Wooden spoon

Time required: $3\frac{1}{2}$–4 hrs

Method

1. Peel pears; cut into quarters and cut out all core.
2. Put vinegar, water, and sugar in pan and bring to boil.
3. Add pears, bring to boil again, and SIMMER 3 hrs, stirring occasionally.
4. Allow to cool, and turn into jar or jars.

Keep the preserve covered to keep out dust, but it need not be sealed. Store in a dry place, and keep an eye on it, as it sometimes grows mould. You can use it right away, but the longer you keep it the richer it tastes. A very little ladled out of the jar, with a blob of whipped cream, makes a luxurious sweet course.

Marmalade

There are innumerable recipes for marmalade, but the one which I use produces a preserve so much nicer than any other I have ever tasted, and is so much easier to do, that I am bound to include it in this book, even though it means using either a hand or an electric MINCER, which not everyone possesses. But if you enjoy marmalade and make enough to last the family a year, it is well worth buying a hand mincer for this purpose alone; otherwise perhaps you can borrow one for an evening.

If you can't get a MINCER, shred the fruit with a sharp knife as finely as you have patience to do. It will still make an excellent marmalade. The important thing is to include the entire fruit and not to discard the pith as in other recipes.

Time required: Using a MINCER makes it much quicker than other methods, but the work should be spread over two days, the fruit being allowed to soften in the water overnight. I am fairly sure that if you went ahead and did it all in one spasm of energy the result would still be very good, but I do advise you to follow the two-day method. Apart from the value to the preserve, doing the work in two stages makes it seem even quicker and easier than it is.

Ingredients (to make about 15 lb.)

8 Seville oranges (bitter)
  ·NOTE: Choose fruit of roughly the same size. Exact weights are unimportant – the result is always good.

2 sweet oranges
2 lemons
8 lb. granulated sugar
8 pts water

Utensils

Packet of jam covers
Jam jars to hold up to 16 lb. preserve
Preserving-pan or large thick saucepan
Mincer
Deep plate
Lemon-squeezer

Measuring jug
Large receptacle to hold sugar
Pointed knife
Small basin
Small saucepan
Strainer
Clean cloths

Time required: Very variable (see above); approx. 1 hr the first day, 3 hrs the second

Two-day method

1. Wash fruit thoroughly and dry.
2. Cut fruit in halves and squeeze out juice, separating the pips into small basin; put juice in preserving-pan.
3. Put all the fruit through the mincer, removing and discarding only the calyx (the small greenish thing resembling a press-stud at the base of the fruit). Put minced fruit into pan with juice.
4. Add 7 pts water.

5. Add the eighth pt to the pips in small basin. Cover pan and bowl with cloths and leave both till next day.

Next day

6. Put pips and water in small saucepan, bring to boil, and boil gently for $\frac{1}{2}$ hr.
7. Put sugar in large receptacle(s) and warm in oven on lowest heat.
8. Strain pips over small basin, pressing gently with wooden spoon. Add the liquor to fruit in preserving-pan and discard pips.
9. Heat fruit gently to boiling point.
10. Add warmed sugar and stir till it dissolves.
11. Boil gently for $1\frac{1}{2}$ hrs, stirring often.
12. Meanwhile, wash jars in hot water, drain, and set to dry in oven at Very Slow, Mark 1, 290° F.
13. Boil marmalade fast for another $\frac{1}{2}$ hr, stirring often (2 hrs altogether). Start TESTING FOR SETTING towards the end of this time.
14. Pot as described at beginning of chapter. Cover at once, or when quite cold.

Lemon Curd

Delicious on brown bread and butter, or to use in lemon meringue pies or tarts.

Ingredients (to make about $2\frac{1}{4}$ lb.)

$\frac{1}{2}$ lb. butter (unsalted or with little salt)
1 lb. caster sugar

4 fresh eggs
2 lemons

Utensils

Packet of jam covers
Small jars to take up to $2\frac{1}{2}$ lb. preserve

Wooden spoon
Grater
Plate

DOUBLE SAUCEPAN or   Fork
  BAIN-MARIE

Time required: $\frac{1}{2}-\frac{3}{4}$ hr

Method

1. Wash jars in hot water, drain, and set to dry in oven at Very Slow, Mark 1, 290° F.
2. Wash lemons well. Grate rind finely, avoiding pith. Then cut in half, squeeze juice and strain.
3. Put butter, sugar, grated rind, and juice of lemons in double saucepan or BAIN-MARIE; heat, stirring occasionally. As soon as butter and sugar have melted, remove top from double saucepan or BAIN-MARIE and allow to cool slightly.
4. Beat eggs with fork sufficiently to mix well. Stir them into the butter and sugar.
5. Return to heat. The water in the bottom container must only SIMMER gently. Stir continuously for about 15 mins., or until the curd begins to thicken. When it ceases to run freely off the spoon, it is ready for potting.
6. Pour straight into pots, or use a small jug. Allow to get quite cold before covering.

NOTE: This is a somewhat rich and mild recipe. A sharper-flavoured curd can be made by using $\frac{1}{4}$ lb. butter and 4 lemons. Owing to the fact that it contains eggs, lemon curd will not keep very long, so do not make too much at once. Keep in a very cool place.

Some Out-of-the-Rut Vegetables and Fruit

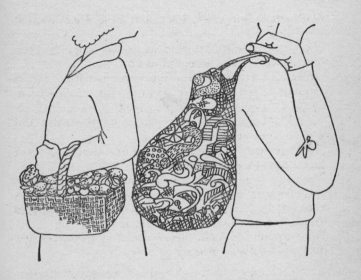

Nowadays, even in small towns and villages, greengrocers often have vegetables and fruit which are strange and exotic-looking, whose names we may or may not know; and although we're willing to try anything once, we feel a bit of a fool asking the assistant what it is and whether you cook it or eat it raw. (He doesn't always know, anyway.)

This is by no means a comprehensive list of all the seasonal fruits and vegetables to be found in shops in London and the great cities. Several are not even unusual and will be familiar to many readers but not, perhaps, to all. Very often these fruits and vegetables are less expensive than you might expect, for you don't need very large quantities. And they will certainly add interest to your table.

Vegetables

Asparagus

Only buy this if it is very fresh. If the heads droop or the ends are brown, it is stale. The small, cheaper ones are often of a better flavour than the fat ones.

To prepare: Scrape the stems downwards from the green part with a sharp knife. Wash the asparagus and tie them in bundles with all the heads at the same level; trim off the ends so that all are the same length.

To cook: The best way is in a vessel deep enough for the stems to be covered in boiling salted water, while the heads are just above the water level, cooking in the steam. There is a special pan made for this, but few of us own one. If you have nothing deep enough, lay the bundles flat in a large saucepan or FISH-KETTLE, cover with boiling salted water, and cook gently until they are tender at the head and at least a third of the way down the stem – about 20 mins. Drain well, handling carefully so as not to damage the tender heads, and serve with melted butter or a FRENCH DRESSING.

You eat them with your fingers, dipping the heads in the melted butter or dressing. FINGER BOWLS should be placed on the table, or alternatively a single plain glass bowl of cold water, perhaps with a flower petal or two floating in it, to dabble greasy fingers in when the asparagus is finished.

Asparagus is also delicious served cold as an HORS D'ŒUVRE with a VINAIGRETTE sauce or MAYONNAISE.

Aubergines (Egg Plant)

This purple-skinned vegetable, usually shaped like an elongated pear, but sometimes roundish, needs no preparation except washing and the removal of the stem.

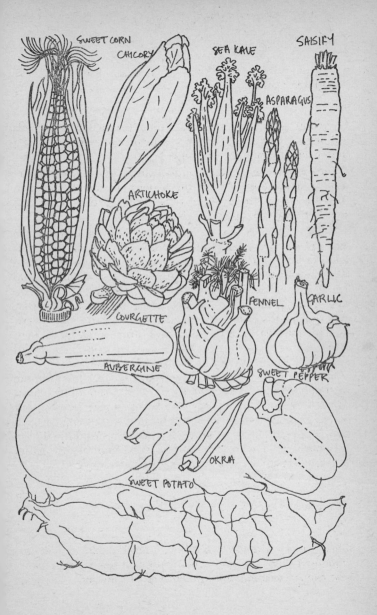

SWEET CORN

CHICORY

SEA KALE

SALSIFY

ASPARAGUS

ARTICHOKE

FENNEL

GARLIC

COURGETTE

AUBERGINE

SWEET PEPPER

OKRA

SWEET POTATO

You can slice it and fry it as an accompaniment to fried liver and bacon or a mixed grill, stew it sliced in tomato sauce, or stuff it and bake it in the oven.

Stuffed Aubergines

Ingredients (to serve 2–4, according to size)

1 plump aubergine	Pepper
1 tablesp. olive oil	Parsley
1 CLOVE OF GARLIC	About 2 rounded tablesp.
1 small onion	BREADCRUMBS (fresh or
2 medium tomatoes	dry)
Salt	½ oz. butter

Utensils

Medium saucepan	Grater
Small saucepan	Plate
Chopping knife and board	Fork
Tablespoon	

Time required: About ½ hr.

Method

1. Set oven to Hot, Mark 7, 425° F.
2. Fill saucepan with water, bring to boil, add a little salt, and boil aubergine gently for 5 mins.
3. Meanwhile, peel onion and garlic and chop finely. Wash and chop parsley – about 2 teasp. Make BREAD-CRUMBS.
4. When aubergine has boiled 5 mins. slice it in half lengthways and carefully scoop out most of the flesh, leaving sufficient in the skins to keep them rigid. (Discard seeds if they are large.)
5. Heat oil in small pan and gently fry onion and garlic for 2 mins. Remove from heat.
6. Wash tomatoes, chop coarsely, and add to onion and garlic. Chop up flesh of aubergine and add to rest of ingredients, together with parsley, salt, and pepper. Mix all well together with fork.

7. Now stuff the two skins of the aubergine with this mixture. Sprinkle tops with BREADCRUMBS, DOT with butter, place in ovenware dish, and bake until browned on top – 10–15 mins.

Chicory

Vaguely resembling the hearts of celery in appearance, formed from tightly packed white leaves yellowish-green at the tips, it has a slightly bitter flavour. It is very refreshing in salads, for which it may be sliced across or the leaves may be pulled off individually. Cooked, it is excellent with any meat or poultry.

To prepare: Wash in salted water, and trim off any brownish leaves.

To braise: The best way to cook it is by melting a little butter or margarine in a thick saucepan, laying the pieces side by side with pepper and salt, a squeeze of lemon, and a couple of tablesp. water, covering closely with a buttered grease-proof paper, putting the lid on the saucepan, and cooking gently for $\frac{1}{2}$–$\frac{3}{4}$ hr, or until they are tender right through. (They go a dark colour in cooking.)

If you do not like the slightly bitter flavour you may BLANCH the chicory by putting it into cold water, bringing to the boil and cooking gently for 5 mins. before proceeding as above. Under *Vegetables* you will find a recipe (p. 65) for cooking chicory with ham and cheese.

Courgettes (Baby Marrows)

Don't peel them, but cut them into thin slices and fry them gently in a little butter or olive oil (with a tablesp. or two of water to prevent them sticking to the saucepan) and a little chopped garlic or onion, parsley, pepper, and salt. Cover the pan and cook very gently, stirring occasionally, for about half an hour. Serve hot or cold.

Fennel

This looks rather like a short, bloated celery, usually with delicate ferny leaves left on it. It has a strong aniseed taste, and a little of the root cut into strips is excellent in a mixed salad, or with tomatoes alone, or in a green salad. You can also cut it up and cook it with butter or olive oil, seasonings, and a little water. The chopped leaves are used in sauces for fish.

Garlic

A small white bulb formed of a number of CLOVES, very pungent and strong-tasting. Used a great deal on the Continent and increasingly in this country, in cooking and in salads. A cut CLOVE rubbed round the salad bowl before putting anything else in it gives the salad an interesting garlicky flavour without being too strong. It has one great disadvantage – it makes the breath smell quite horrible; so don't eat it if you are going to a dance or taking part in amateur theatricals.

Globe Artichokes

These are really the flower buds: the CHOKE (the part you don't eat) develops in the normal course of events into a handsome purple thistle-like flower.

Allow one per person, or half each if they are the very large ones. Wash them thoroughly, then cut off the stalk and coarse outer leaves. Cook in boiling salted water for between 30 and 45 mins. (according to size). You can tell if they are done by pulling the outer leaves, which come off easily when the artichoke is ready. Drain well, upside down, for a minute or two, serve either hot with melted butter or cold with a vinaigrette sauce (or oil and lemon) or mayonnaise.

You eat them by pulling off the leaves one by one with your fingers, dipping them in the VINAIGRETTE, and eating the thick, fleshy part at the bottom. The rest of the leaf is discarded (you need an extra plate for these). Eventually you come to the 'bottom' or 'heart', which is the choicest part; but you must first remove the CHOKE with a knife. Eat the bottom with a small spoon and plenty of sauce. (Don't get any of the CHOKE in your mouth. The name is apt – it is like having a mouthful of fine pins.)

Artichoke hearts are sometimes served alone, with a simple FRENCH DRESSING (p. 112) as an hors d'œuvre, but these are usually the tinned kind. In Italy, where the artichokes are smaller and more tender, they cook and eat the entire vegetable in various delicious ways.

When serving artichokes, individual finger bowls should be placed on the table, half filled with cold water (and perhaps a flower petal or two) for the guests to dabble their fingers in when they have finished. If you have no finger-bowls or anything that would serve the purpose, a reasonably attractive 'communal' bowl will do very well.

Okra or Ladies' Fingers

These little angular seed-pods should be young and firm or are probably not worth buying. Wash and dry them thoroughly, break rather than cut off the stems, parboil them in slightly salted water for a very few minutes, then drain well and fry them in butter. Eat very hot with plenty of salt and pepper. Some people like them with tomato sauce. They can be used as an accompaniment to fish, poultry or meat.

Pimentoes
(Sweet Peppers, Capsicums)

They can be green yellow, or red. The green are most commonly seen in our shops. You can buy them by the pound, and they vary greatly in size. You can buy just one – pick out a nice, glossy, unwrinkled one. It can be shredded raw, or cooked for a few minutes in a little boiling, salted water, and then used in any kind of salad, particularly in Spanish Salad for which the red are best. The flavour is very distinctive, slightly earthy. Don't use too much at a time.

You can also stuff whole pimentoes and serve them with meat, particularly lamb or veal, or alone as a supper or lunch dish; or you can cut them in quarters, season them with salt and pepper, and bake them in a little olive oil for about half an hour in a moderate oven, or at the bottom of the oven while you are roasting a joint.

NOTE: *All* seeds and pith from the inside must always be cut away.

Stuffed Pimentoes

Ingredients (to serve 4)

4 large pimentoes (choose round ones rather than elongated)
3 tablesp. olive oil or butter
1 rounded tablesp. rice
4 oz. ham or cooked chicken (or scraps of cold meat)

1 small rasher of bacon (preferably streaky)
1 small onion or SHALLOT
1 egg
2 tomatoes
Salt, Pepper
Parsley

Utensils

Ovenware baking dish	Small knife
Chopping board and knife	Scissors
Fork	2 small saucepans
Cup	Clean cloth
Strainer	

Time required: About 1½ hrs

Method

1. Wash and cook rice as for plain boiled rice (p. 104).
2. Set oven to Moderate, Mark 4, 355° F.
3. Wash and dry pimentoes and slice off the tops about one-third of the way down. Cut out all seeds and pith.
4. Cut bacon into tiny pieces. Peel and chop onion or SHALLOT finely. Chop ham or chicken very small (or put through a mincer). SKIN tomatoes and chop small. Wash and chop parsley.
5. Heat a small tablesp. olive oil in saucepan and gently fry onion and bacon for 2 mins. When soft, remove from heat and add ham or chicken, rice, and tomatoes.
6. Beat egg lightly in cup and add to other ingredients. Add parsley and salt and pepper. Mix all well with fork.
7. Fill the pimentoes with the mixture and replace the 'lid' on each. Spoon the rest of the olive oil over them, put them in the ovenware dish, and bake on centre shelf in oven for 30–45 mins. until soft. Serve at once.

These can also be served cold as an HORS D'ŒUVRE. The rice may be replaced by BREADCRUMBS and the stuffing varied with grated cheese, chopped anchovies, or other variations on this theme.

Salsify

Can be black or white. It looks like an extremely elongated carrot and has a delicious nutty flavour. Scrape off the skin, and put the salsify in cold water with a little lemon juice or vinegar to prevent discoloration. Boil them in a little salted water, and a dash of lemon juice or vinegar, until tender – about half an hour. Serve with melted butter. (Goes with any meat.)

Seakale

Seakale also looks a little like celery but does not taste anything like it. It has white stems, pale mauvish leaves, and a most delicate flavour. Trim off the coarse ends of the stalks. Wash what is left and cook gently with very little water and a little lemon juice. Serve with melted butter. It is also good raw in salads.

Sweet Corn

Originally an American habit, eating 'Corn-on-the-Cob' has become very popular in Britain. The cobs should be gold in colour and tender enough to exude a milky fluid if you press your nail into a seed. If they are old and coarse, they are not worth eating. Strip off the outer sheath and 'tassel' and cook them in boiling, salted water for 10–15 mins. Eat with plenty of melted butter. You can buy special picks to hold the cob, but two forks will do very well if you don't like getting your fingers greasy.

Sweet Potato

This originally tropical root vegetable, like a large, coarse-looking, pinkish potato in appearance, is not in fact related to our potato but may be treated in similar ways. The simplest way to cook it is to bake or boil it in its skin, then peel and mash it with salt, pepper and butter; or with butter and a little sugar. You may also parboil it in slightly salted water, then slice and sauté it in butter or dripping. You may even treat it exactly like the common potato and make chips of it, or you may peel it, cut it into largish pieces and roast it round the joint, as you would parsnips. For sweet potato soups or even sweets, I suggest you consult an American recipe book.

Avocado Pears

These dark green pear-like fruits have a white, creamy flesh with a subtle taste and an enormous round stone (which can be grown, with patience, into a quite presentable pot plant).

Choose the fruit carefully – it should yield to gentle thumb pressure. A black discoloration of the skin is of no importance. The best way is to buy the fruit while still hard and keep it until it is ripened to your taste. Allow half a pear per head.

You can eat it as an HORS D'ŒUVRE. You can spoon out the flesh just as it is, with a squeeze of lemon juice or a simple French dressing; or make a VINAIGRETTE based on a FRENCH DRESSING, with lots of finely chopped garlic, onion, gherkin, tomato, parsley, and salt and pepper. Some people mix the flesh with yolk of hard-boiled eggs and make stuffed eggs. And you can make stuffed avocados, by filling the hollows left by the stones with shrimps in MAYONNAISE.

Lichees

These little fruits have a hard, brownish shell which you peel off with your fingers. Inside is a bluish-grey fleshy fruit of the most delectable flavour. Just eat them.

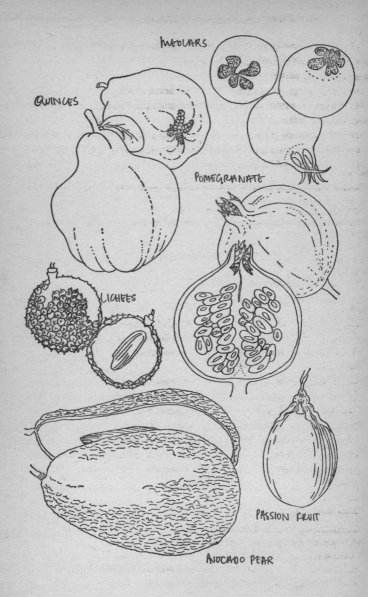

MEDLARS

QUINCES

POMEGRANATE

LICHEES

PASSION FRUIT

AVOCADO PEAR

Medlars

They look like tiny, leathery brown apples, with a crown of dried, spiky sepals. You don't eat them until they are 'bletted', that is mushy (some people call it 'rotten'). A few connoisseurs dote on them; but most people find them rather horrid.

Passion-Fruit (Grenadilla)

Plum-like, greenish-purple fruit, very seedy. Eat it alone or in fruit salad.

Pink Grapefruit

These are exactly like the others, but are said to be more so. Amusing for a party.

Pomegranate

This fruit can be eaten any way you please – they are all a bit tedious, as the innumerable fleshy cells contain a great many seeds as well as lots of the refreshing juice. (The leathery skin is not edible.) Cut the fruit across and take a teaspoon to it; or into four and bite into it. Some people squeeze and pinch the fruit to crush the inside, then pierce a hole in the skin and squeeze the juice straight into their mouths. I have not tried this myself.

T–H

Pumpkin

You can usually buy this in pieces, and there are a great many ways of using it. It can be cooked in any of the ways in which we usually cook marrow; it can be fried, made into soup, baked in a pie. To fry pumpkin, cut it into manageable pieces, discarding any seeds, and fry gently in butter or oil for 20–30 mins.

Quinces

Look a bit like golden pears. Some people like them stewed, but they have rather a floury texture. One, cut up with the apples, is good in an apple pie. They make quite a pleasant jam, and a superb jelly which you can eat with meat like redcurrant jelly, or on bread and butter. (A recipe for Quince Jelly will be found on p. 184.)

A Word about Cheeses

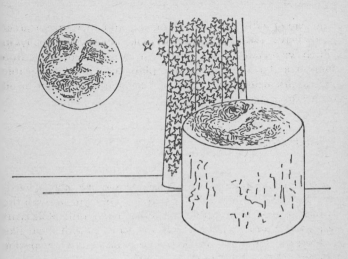

The French, who are without doubt the most discriminating eaters in the world as well as the best cooks, eat far fewer puddings and sweets than we do, often following the main course of their meal with cheese and afterwards fruit.

Incidentally, if they do serve a sweet course, it comes *after* the cheese, not before it as in this country. This is a matter of national custom and habit, and I don't think there is any particular merit in either their way or ours; the cheese is the thing. It can be very rewarding to serve a board of assorted cheeses in place of the usual suet pudding or tin of pineapple and much better for our health and beauty – though to be honest I must confess that I have not noticed that the French people are markedly superior to us in either, so perhaps our bad eating habits cancel each other out.

Even among the experts opinions differ on whether or not cheese should be kept in a refrigerator. My own experience is that it is perfectly all right, provided you take it out several hours before you use it. Cheese must be kept cool and covered, but not without air or it quickly goes mouldy. On the other hand, if it is entirely open to the air it goes dry and sometimes rancid.

We have an excellent variety of cheeses in this country. We also import a great number, and if you have access to a delicatessen shop or large grocery where you can obtain foreign as well as British cheeses, you will find it well worth while to be as adventurous in buying as your purse will permit. Admittedly some cheeses are very expensive, but by no means all.

To experience their full flavour, cheeses should sometimes be eaten alone, with a knife and fork, instead of with bread or biscuits, and butter is often unnecessary.

This is just a note to remind you of a very few of the cheeses easily obtainable. There are a great many more, including herb-flavoured cream cheeses, smoked or other processed cheeses, which come and go in the shops, and I apologize if I have omitted your favourite.

British Cheeses

Caerphilly. An excellent mild cheese from Wales.

Cheddar. The good old stand-by. Can be first-rate; can also be of the variety known as 'mouse-trap' which is *just* edible. Slightly stale Cheddar is the best cheese for cooking, unless you can obtain fresh Parmesan and grate it yourself. There are various imitations of our native Cheddar: Canadian, New Zealand, Irish, etc. They vary in quality and pungency and must be tried.

Cheshire. A reddish-orange cheese, crumbly in texture, fairly mild in flavour.

Double Gloucester. Rather similar to Cheshire, but milder.

Lancashire. Very mild and crumbly. Not much individuality, but cheap.

Stilton. A king among cheeses – none better, but whenever you can you must eat it in a restaurant or pub cut from the whole cheese. It is incomparably better than if bought in small pieces. If you can buy a whole one and share it with your neighbours and friends as is often done at Christmas, good luck to you!

Wensleydale. A good, solid Yorkshire cheese with a sound personality of its own. When you start, you find you can eat any amount of it.

Continental Cheeses

Bel Paese. A sweet, mild, soft Italian cheese with a slightly rubbery texture. Delicious eaten with a fresh pear. Unfortunately, it is often only obtainable here in minute, mouth-size individual packs.

Brie. A flat, circular French cheese, about 14 in. in diameter, usually sold on a bed of straw. Soft and creamy and not too strong. (It can also be bought in separately-packed wedges.)

Camembert. Probably the most famous of all French cheeses. Similar in texture to Brie, but *much* stronger. Has to be 'ripe' (that is, beginning to be runny) to be at its best; some people find it too 'high' at this stage. It certainly announces its presence unmistakably, but if you like it at all, you'll like it this way.

Danish or Swedish Blue. The least expensive of the blue-vein cheeses, creamy and rich, but can be harsh.

Demi-sel. A small, soft creamy cheese wrapped in foil, firmer-textured than the Petit-Suisse and not so expensive. To be spread.

Edam. The Dutch cheese with the red rind. Good, every-day fare.

Emmenthal. This cheese is similar to Gruyère, but rather finer and the holes or 'eyes' are larger.

Gorgonzola. A very strongly flavoured blue cheese from Italy – an aristocratic cheese.

Gouda. Dutch cheese, slightly softer and milder than Edam.

Gruyère. The one with small holes or 'eyes' in it. This cheese and Emmenthal are of a different texture from all the others – very smooth and firm. Some people prefer them to all other cheeses, while some find them a bit soapy.

Jarlsberg. A pleasant and cheap Scandinavian cheese somewhat resembling an inferior Gruyère.

Parmesan. An extremely hard Italian cheese, made from goat's milk. The best for cooking. You can buy it ready grated; but if you don't object to hard work it is preferable to keep a piece by you and grate it as needed. It keeps a very long time.

Petit-Suisse. Delicious little soft creamy cheese, sometimes bought in boxes of three, each in its individual paper wrapping. Wonderful eaten with caster sugar as a dessert or try it with salt and pepper. Eat it with a spoon.

Roquefort. An exquisitely flavoured cheese made from the milk of ewes in the lambing season at the village of Roquefort in the Cévennes, France. Exceedingly expensive.

Tôme de Savoi. Sometimes known as *tôme aux raisins*. A mild creamy cheese, fairly solid, with a black crust made from grape pips which gives it a special flavour.

Curd, Milk, or Cottage Cheese. Different names for a simple cheese which can be bought or can be made at home simply by allowing milk to go sour in a shallow dish until it clots and then hanging it in a muslin bag for the whey to drain off. The remaining curd can then be eaten as it is with salt, or made more interesting by the addition of chopped CHIVES or other herbs.

Liptauer Cheese. A savoury cottage cheese, useful to spread on bread, toast, biscuits, or crispbreads as a snack or as part of a buffet meal. (See recipe opposite.)

Liptauer Cheese

Ingredients

4 oz. curd cheese
4 oz. butter
2 fillets of anchovy
1 level dessertsp. CARAWAY
SEEDS
1 level dessertsp. CHIVES (or
very finely chopped spring
onion or SHALLOT)

1 level dessertsp. CAPERS
1 level dessertsp. PAPRIKA
1 teasp. MADE MUSTARD
(English)
½ teasp. salt
Pinch of celery salt

Utensils

Sieve or strainer
Chopping knife and board
Dessert spoon

Teaspoon
Medium basin
Wooden spoon

Time required: About ½ hr

Method

1. CREAM butter with wooden spoon in bowl until quite soft.
2. Drain as much oil as possible from anchovies and chop them finely.
3. Chop CAPERS and CHIVES (or alternative).
4. Sieve the cheese and beat it into the butter a little at a time. When mixture is soft and creamy, add rest of ingredients and mix well until all is well incorporated. The Liptauer should be a good orange-pink colour and very savoury. Add more PAPRIKA if you think it necessary. Serve piled in a bowl or spread on biscuits.

A Few Suggested Menus for Entertaining

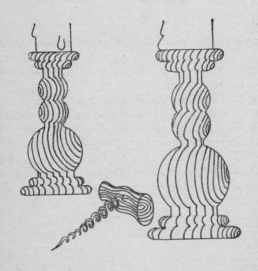

I hope that the recipes in this book will encourage and help you to entertain your friends and relations, either formally or informally as the spirit moves you.

Parties which offer only potato crisps, or sandwiches, or bread and cheese have a dreary feeling from the start. My view is the old-fashioned one that the nicest way to show affection to your friends and courtesy to acquaintances is to put yourself out to entertain them, offering the best you have in food and drink, no matter how simple it may be. A dish of hot dripping toast prepared by yourself and pleasingly served will give far more pleasure (and nourishment) to your guests than a boring plate of shop biscuits, and cost no more.

It's a good rule never to give a party without offering

something you have gone to some trouble to prepare, and let hospitality come into its own again.

Items marked with an asterisk* can be entirely or partially prepared in advance and re-heated if they are to be served hot. Some may be cooked the previous day. Recipes for all these menus are included in this book.

Light Lunch

Menu

Speedy soup
*Fish cakes with watercress and tomato sauce
Fruit

Order of Preparation

1. Set table.
2. Put dishes and plates to warm.
3. Make fish cakes, but do not fry.
4. Make sauce; set aside in pan.
5. Wash and dry water-cress.
6. Prepare soup, but do not finish.
7. Fry fish cakes, and keep hot.
8. Finish soup and serve. Set sauce to reheat on lowest heat.
9. Add watercress to fish-cakes at last minute.

Ham omelette
*Tomato salad
Cheese and fruit

1. Set table.
2. Put dishes and plates to warm.
3. Prepare salad.
4. Make omelette and serve.

Menu	Order of Preparation
*Cream of tomato soup Cauliflower *au gratin* with hard-boiled eggs Fruit	1. Make soup. When cooked, remove from heat. 2. Make cauliflower AU GRATIN with eggs. 3. Before finishing under grill, set soup to reheat gently. 4. Serve when it reaches boiling point, and keep cauliflower hot.
Stuffed pimentoes *Crème caramel* (Caramel custard) Fruit	1. Make *crème caramel* early in morning or previous day. 2. Set table. 3. Put dishes and plates to warm. 4. Make stuffed pimentoes.
Smoked haddock in lemon-flavoured sauce Apple salad	1. Set table. 2. Put dishes and plates to warm. 3. Make apple salad. 4. Cook haddock.

Guests to Dinner

Cheese and biscuits or a choice of brown, white or crispbread may be included in any of the menus.

ADVANCED

Menu	Order of Preparation
*Stuffed eggs Mixed grill, with tomatoes, mushrooms, chips, and any green vegetable	1. Make fool early (or previous day). 2. Make stuffed eggs early (or previous day).

Menu	*Order of Preparation*

Fruit, or *gooseberry fool

3. Set table.
4. Put dishes and plates to warm.
5. Prepare green vegetable.
6. Cook grill and chips.
7. Dish up vegetable and grill, and keep hot.
8. Re-heat oil for chips, turn down heat, and cover.
9. Eat first course. While someone else clears, finish chips and serve.

Les carbonnades flamandes
  (beef stewed in beer)
  with mashed potatoes
 Green salad
*Jam puffs

1. Make jam puffs early (or previous day).
2. Make *carbonnades flamandes*.
3. Set table.
4. Put dishes and plates to warm.
5. Prepare salad, but do not dress.
6. Cook potatoes.
7. Set puffs to reheat in moderate oven, if wanted hot.
8. Dress salad.

ADVANCED

Julienne soup
 Pot-roasted veal with
   mashed potatoes and
   braised chicory
Poire Hélène

1. If making own ice-cream make early in morning.
2. Cook pears early in day.
3. Set veal to cook.
4. Make soup, and set aside when cooked.
5. Make chocolate sauce, and set aside.
6. Set table.

Menu	*Order of Preparation*

<table>
<tr><td></td><td>

7. Put dishes and plates to warm.
8. Cook vegetables.
9. Set sauce to re-heat in BAIN-MARIE.
10. Re-heat soup.
11. Dish up meat and vegetables and keep hot.
</td></tr>
</table>

*Cucumber salad with yoghourt Curried chicken with rice and chutney *Oranges with sugar	1. Make curry. 2. Prepare cucumber with salt. 3. Prepare oranges with sugar. 4. Set table. 5. Put dishes and plates to warm. 6. Cook rice. 7. Dress salad with yoghourt. 8. Dish up curry and rice, and keep hot.
*Minestrone soup Skate with black butter sauce and boiled potatoes Orleans pudding	1. Make soup early (or previous day). 2. Make pudding, and set to cook. 3. Set table. 4. Cook potatoes. 5. Put dishes and plates to heat. 6. Cook fish, dish up, and keep hot. 7. Dish up potatoes, and keep hot. 8. Re-heat soup.

Menu	Order of Preparation
	9. Serve soup and eat. While someone else clears, dish up pudding, and keep hot.
	10. Serve fish.
*Prawn cocktail *Wiener Schnitzel* with *sauté* potatoes and green beans, or spring carrots (in season), or cauliflower sprigs, or peas, or broccoli *Fruit salad	1. Cook potatoes, and allow to get cold.
	2. Prepare fruit salad, and chill.
	3. Set table.
	4. Prepare vegetables.
	5. Prepare meat and potatoes for cooking.
	6. Make prawn cocktails, and chill.
	7. Put dishes and plates to warm.
	8. Cook schnitzels, potatoes, and vegetables, and keep hot.

Informal Parties for any Number up to 20

Menu	To Drink
*Minestrone soup *Sausage rolls or pasties (hot) *Fruit salad	Hot spiced cider Lemonade Mineral waters
*Onion soup *Tomato cheese spread, on hot buttered toast made at party *Slabs of gingerbread and fruit loaf Fruit	Cider Apple juice Mineral waters

Menu

*Spaghetti bolognese
  Green salad
*Ice cream with hot chocolate sauce

Drink Suggestions

Pleasant and cheap Italian red wine – Valpolicella.
Cider
Apple juice
Lemonade
(If wine is permitted, for older guests, Chianti or Valpolicella are suitable pleasant and cheap Italian wines.)

*Hot Frankfurter sausages.
    Put them in water just off the boil and leave 10 mins. Prick them first with a fork, or they will burst
*Potato salad
*Tomato salad
*Chocolate mousse or fruit salad

Cider
Apple juice
Beer.

  Risotto
  Green salad
*Fruit salad

Wine – red, white or rosé. I would choose the latter.

Simple Buffet Party

Almost all the suggested food may be partly or entirely prepared the day before the party. I suggest that this should be done whenever possible, to allow you plenty of time for finishing touches, table arrangements, and jobs such as fruit salad (which does not improve with keeping overnight) which must be done on the day. Allow yourself at least an hour for dressing and titivating, too. And don't get flustered: none of your guests is going to mind if you are still putting sprigs of parsley on the sandwiches when they arrive, as long as your hair is not still in rollers.

A cup of hot or iced soup – according to the weather – is always appreciated as a starter. So is a small cup of good coffee when the eating is over.

An assortment of cold cooked meats may be accompanied by any of the following.

Small sausage pasties (hot or cold)
Stuffed eggs
Cheese straws
Tomato-cheese-spread on water biscuits
Liptauer cheese on crispbread or thin rye bread
Salads – Spanish, green bean, tomato, mushroom
Chocolate *profiteroles*
Meringues
Fruit salad
Chocolate mousse in paper cups

Cider or Claret cup might be served as well as or instead of more potent wines and spirits.

Bottled apple juice is popular with teetotallers.

VOL-AU-VENTS (small cases of puff pastry with a savoury filling) are appreciated at any kind of party. You may either make them yourself, exactly as you make jam puffs (p. 120), or buy them ready prepared from a good pastrycook. Make your own filling of chopped shrimps, mushrooms, chicken and ham, etc., in a creamy white sauce (fairly thick white sauce – p. 106 – with a little cream added), and heat them in a moderate oven before serving.

Glossary

ALLSPICE. A spice from Jamaica looking like a large peppercorn, supposed to combine flavours of cinnamon, nutmeg, and cloves. Can also be used ground.

ARROWROOT. A starch prepared from the arrowroot plant, used mainly for thickening.

ASBESTOS MAT. Asbestos will not burn. When heat of burner or hot-plate is insufficiently low, mats made of it are used under saucepans to keep food gently simmering. (Not always suitable with North Sea gas.)

ASPIC JELLY. A clear, savoury jelly used to garnish cold dishes or make savoury moulds. Can be made at home or bought in packet form.

AU GRATIN. Any dish covered with a sauce and breadcrumbs, cooked in the oven or browned under grill. Often has cheese in recipe or mixed with crumbs. Served in the dish in which it was cooked.

AU NATUREL. Food served raw, or cooked in the simplest possible way.

BAIN-MARIE. Vessel of hot water in which smaller pans or basins are stood to heat or keep hot; an alternative to DOUBLE SAUCE-PAN.

BASKET, CHIP. A wire basket on a long handle, made to fit inside a deep frying pan or saucepan; for frying potatoes or other food in deep fat and to facilitate lifting it out.

BASTE. To spoon hot fat or liquid over food during cooking, usually in oven.

BEARD. Attachment thread of some shell-fish; gills of oyster.

BEATER, ROTARY. See ROTARY BEATER.

BLANCH. 1. To dip food first into boiling water for a short time and then into cold, to facilitate removal of skin. Almonds are blanched by pouring boiling water on to them and leaving them for several minutes, when the skins can easily be removed. 2. To blanch meat, put it into cold water and bring gently to boil, skimming off any scum which rises. Remove and cool quickly by putting into cold water.

BOUQUET GARNI. A bunch of herbs, usually thyme, parsley, and bay leaf.

BOWLS, FINGER. See FINGER BOWLS.

BRAISE. A method of slow cooking. Meat or vegetables are usually browned first in a little fat and then stewed in covered pan.

BREADCRUMBS. *Fresh breadcrumbs* are made by rubbing stale bread on a grater; finer ones can be made by rubbing it round a colander with a piece of crust. *Dry breadcrumbs* or raspings are made by crushing with a rolling pin, grating or putting through a mincer bread which has been dried in a slow oven.

BUCKLING. A kind of smoked herring, as kippers or bloaters.

BUTTER BEANS, GOLDEN. See GOLDEN BUTTER BEANS.

BUTTER, NUT OF. See NUT OF BUTTER.

CAPERS. Flower buds of a shrub from Southern Europe, pickled. Used in sauces or as a garnish for fish or meat.

CAPSICUM. See p. 198.

CARAWAY SEEDS. Seeds of a plant with a very strong and distinctive flavour, used in cakes, notably Seed Cake, and in some Continental breads and other dishes.

CAYENNE PEPPER. A hot, red pepper made from chillies. Use sparingly.

CHEESE SAUCE. See p. 107.

CHERVIL. Herb used in salads, soups, for fish sauces, etc.

CHIP BASKET. See BASKET, CHIP.

CHIVES. The grass-like leaves of a herb with a mild onion flavour. Always used fresh. Easily grown in a garden or pot, but not often found in shops.

CHOKE. Centre part of GLOBE ARTICHOKE.

CINNAMON. The inner bark of a tree growing in the East Indies. It is used rolled into little STICKS, or ground. For flavouring.

CLOVE OF GARLIC. One of the small bulbs making up compound bulb of garlic. Vary enormously in size. An average clove is about the size of an almond. If larger, divide. Beware of overdoing it.

CLOVES. A spice – actually the dried bud of a tropical tree.

CONDIMENTS. Something used to give relish to food: seasonings, spices, etc.

CORRECT SEASONING. This means tasting the food and then adding salt, pepper, or any other condiment you think necessary.

CREAM. To beat, usually with wooden spoon, until soft and creamy.

CREAM, WHIPPED. See WHIPPED CREAM.

CROÛTONS. Small squares or cubes of toast or fried bread. See p. 15.

DAB. Small flatfish caught in rivers near the sea. Slips (tiny soles) are sometimes called dabs.

DARIOLE MOULDS. Small moulds shaped like flowerpots.

DEEP FRY. To fry by immersing the food completely in deep fat. Often best done by means of a wire frying-basket.

DICE. Small cubes of bread, vegetables, cheese, etc. To dice is to cut them into such cubes. An easy way to dice an onion or large carrot or turnip is to hold it in one hand and score it deeply across with a sharp knife in the other hand; then score across at right angles, then slice across so that the top slice falls into cubes. Repeat until all is cut into dice. *Be careful not to cut your hand:* the last slice has to be done on a hard surface.

DOT. Put small spots (usually of butter) over the surface of a dish.

DOUBLE SAUCEPAN. Two saucepans really, the lower to contain water and the top, smaller half to fit inside it so that food can be cooked in it in the indirect heat of the boiling water below and need never actually boil.

DREDGE. Sprinkle. A DREDGER is a container with a perforated lid, for dredging food with flour or sugar.

DRESSING, FRENCH. See p. 112.

ESCALOPE. Thin slice of meat cut from the fillet (usually the top of the leg).

FINGER-BOWLS. These are rarely seen except at formal dinners, but are really necessary (at least when entertaining) if anything, such as asparagus, artichokes, and some fruits, is eaten with the fingers. They are usually small individual glass bowls half filled with water. Sometimes a small flower such as a violet, or a few petals, are floated in the water for a decorative effect. If finger-bowls are not available, a single bowl of water placed in the centre of the table is a suitable substitute for the diners to dabble their greasy fingers in.

FISH-KETTLE. A pan, usually oval, containing a removable strainer, designed for steaming or boiling fish and lifting it out without breaking it. Has many other uses.

FISH-SLICE. A usually rectangular perforated blade on a long handle, for turning or lifting fish or other food from pan.

FLAKY PASTRY. Makes a light, crisp, flaky crust for pies, sausage-rolls, etc. A little more difficult to make than rough puff pastry, but used much in the same way.

FLUTE. To make a frilled edge by pressing down with thumb or forefinger all along the outer edge of pie or tart, before baking. Knocking up the pastry between each flute with the back of a knife held in the other hand is a help.

FOLD (IN). Usually applied to flour. Really CUT AND FOLD, for mixing without beating. A metal spoon is used, which cuts down through the mixture and folds the flour over the rest, continuing gently until all is well incorporated.

FORCING-BAG. A cone-shaped bag, usually of canvas, with inserted metal tubes for forcing out icing, mashed potato, whipped cream, mayonnaise, etc., into decorative forms and patterns. A metal syringe may also be used, or even a cone made of heavy paper with the tip cut in different patterns.

FRENCH DRESSING. The classic salad dressing. See p. 112.

GARLIC. Bulbous root divided into numerous smaller bulbs or CLOVES, with strong pungent flavour. Much used in Continental cooking and increasingly here.

GARLIC SALT. Salt flavoured with garlic. A substitute when garlic is not available.

GARNISH. Decorate or embellish.

GLACÉ CHERRY OR OTHER FRUIT. Candied.

GLAZE. To give a shiny surface by brushing with white of egg, beaten egg, or milk before cooking. For cold meat or fish dishes, a glaze is made with ASPIC JELLY.

GLOBE ARTICHOKES. See p. 196.

GOLDEN BUTTER BEANS. Small golden-yellow beans, to be found in most seed catalogues, grown much on the Continent but not often here, and only occasionally seen in our shops. Recommended for those who can grow their own vegetables. Easily grown, labour-saving, and delicious.

HORS D'ŒUVRE. Meaning 'digression'. Dishes served at the beginning of the meal as appetizers. Can be one dish or a selection of small titbits.

HULL. Outer covering of fruit; pod, calyx of strawberry. To remove this.

KNEAD. To work a dough lightly with knuckles, bringing the outside up and over towards the centre – the object being to get a smooth texture.

LINE. Make a greaseproof paper lining for a cake-tin, to prevent the cake from burning. See p. 155.

MACE. The dried outer covering of the nutmeg. Used in 'blades', or ground, for pickles and for both sweet and savoury dishes.

MADE MUSTARD. Mustard not in powder form but already mixed to a creamy consistency with water (English) or vinegar and seasoning (French).

MASHER. A tool for mashing potatoes or other foods, with a flat usually oval head containing angled perforations through which the food is forced.

MAYONNAISE. A thick creamy dressing for fish, salads, etc. See p. 109.

MELT, To melt onions, garlic, etc., in butter means to soften in the butter without colouring them, or causing only the very slightest colouring.

MEUNIÈRE. A method of cooking fish. See p. 23.

MINCER. A hand or electric tool for mincing meat or other foods finely.

MINESTRONE. A vegetable soup. See p. 4.

NUT. A piece (usually of butter) about the size of a small walnut.

NUTMEG. A spice – the very aromatic seed of the East Indian nutmeg tree. Used in sweet and savoury dishes.

ONION, LARGE. An onion weighing upwards of 6 oz.

PALETTE KNIFE. A wide flexible blade for turning or lifting food. (Same as SPATULA.)

PANADA. A thick paste made from flour and a liquid. Used as a binding. Also the basis of soufflés and *choux* pastry.

PAPRIKA. A mild-flavoured red powder made from capsicums, used for flavouring and colouring savoury dishes, particularly Hungarian Goulash.

PASTA. General term (Italian) for spaghetti, macaroni, and all the numerous other forms of 'pastes' made from wheaten or semolina flour.

PEEL, WHOLE. Candied orange, lemon, and other fruit peel in large pieces, not chopped.

PEPPER MILL. A small wooden mill for table or kitchen, for grinding fresh pepper.

PEPPERCORNS. Dried whole berries of the black pepper plant, which are ground to form pepper in powdered form. Black pepper is the stronger and is dried unripe berries; white pepper is the ripe berries.

POACH. To cook in liquid just below boiling point.

POD, VANILLA. See VANILLA POD.

PURÉE. Vegetables or fruit after having been cooked and rubbed through a sieve.

ROTARY BEATER or EGG WHISK. A beater or whisk with blades which revolve by means of a small wheel turned by a handle.

ROUX. A mixture of fat and flour cooked together for a few minutes. Used as a basis for sauces or to thicken soups, stews, etc.

RUB IN. Rub flour and fat together between the finger-tips until mixture resembles fine breadcrumbs.

RUST. Term used to describe the hard edges of bacon rashers opposite to the rind, which should be trimmed away before cooking.

SALAD SHAKER. A wire or plastic globular double basket which opens and in which washed salad can be swung and shaken to dry it.

SAUCE-BOAT. A boat-shaped dish for serving sauces or gravy.

SAUCE TARTARE. See p. 111.

SAUTÉ. Tossed (literally 'jumped') in very little hot fat until lightly browned all over.

SCORE. Make a shallow incision or slash.

SEASONED FLOUR. Flour already seasoned with salt and pepper. (It is a good idea to keep some in a dredger.)

SEASONING. Salt, pepper, and any other flavourings.

SEPARATE YOLK FROM WHITE. Take two cups. Knock egg sharply on edge of one, to break shell as cleanly as possible into two halves. Open up the halves and let the white drop between them into one cup. Tip yolk from one half-shell to the other once or twice, to release any remaining white into the cup. Some people like to remove the 'eye' of the egg, which is easily done with a piece of eggshell – this is also the best way to remove from the white any yolk which may have fallen into it if the yolk breaks, which will prevent the white from being easily beaten stiff.

SHALLOT. Similar to onion but much smaller and milder.

SIMMER. To cook just below boiling point, so that only an occasional bubble breaks on the surface.

SKIN TOMATOES. You can skin tomatoes by holding them on the point of a knife over a gas flame for a moment or two, when the skin can be split and peeled off. More foolproof, put them in water which is just off the boil and leave for a few seconds.

SLIPS. Tiny soles. (Sometimes called dabs, though these are really a different fish. See DABS.)

SOUFFLÉ DISH. A rather deep round dish, often ridged outside, of earthenware or other ovenware, primarily for baking soufflés.

SOUR MILK. Used for scones and some cakes and puddings and in some Continental cookery. Also to make cottage cheese. You can sour milk deliberately, by the addition of 1–2 tablesp. lemon juice to a pint.

SPATULA. Same as PALETTE KNIFE.

STICK OF CINNAMON. See CINNAMON.

STOCK. Liquid used as foundation for soups, stews, etc., and made from bones, meat trimmings, vegetables, etc.; or from fish and fish trimmings for a fish stock, and so on. Good-quality meat or chicken extracts in cube form are a good substitute for the hard-pressed cook.

STRING. To remove fruit from stems of cluster, e.g. black or red currants (p. 182). Also to remove coarse fibres from edges of green beans.

TARRAGON VINEGAR. Vinegar flavoured with Tarragon.

TEST FOR A SET. See p. 179.

TEST WITH SKEWER. Insert skewer into thickest part of cake. If it comes out perfectly clean, the cake is cooked.

THYME. An aromatic herb, used fresh or dry. One of the three essentials in a BOUQUET GARNI.

TUREEN. Deep serving-dish for soup, with lid.

VANILLA ESSENCE. Liquid vanilla flavouring, concentrated. For puddings, cakes, etc.

VANILLA POD. Fruit of the vanilla bean, dried; used whole to flavour custards, etc. (See also page 133.)

VANILLA SUGAR. Caster or granulated sugar kept in a jar with a vanilla pod so that the sugar is ready-flavoured when required for puddings, cakes, and custards.

VINAIGRETTE. A sauce based on FRENCH DRESSING (p. 112).

VOL-AU-VENT. Small pastry cases made of extremely light puff pastry (literally 'fly in the wind') and filled with creamed chicken, mushrooms, shrimps, or other savoury fillings.

WHIPPED CREAM. Use double cream, add a pinch of sugar and beat, preferably with a ROTARY BEATER, until cream is thick. Add sugar to taste.

WHOLE PEEL. See PEEL.

WINE VINEGAR. Vinegar made from wine rather than from malt or acetic acid, and of a finer quality.

YOGHOURT. Milk treated with certain bacteria to produce a sourish creamy liquid, very refreshing eaten alone or with sugar or as an accompaniment to stewed fruit. Also used in cooking, sometimes in place of sour cream.

Index

a Penguin Handbook

The Shelter Cookery Book

A collection of recipes from famous people

Edited by Betty Falk

You may know a better recipe book than this. You'll never find one with more distinguished authors.

Just look at the Contents List. Here are the Prime Minister and the Archbishop of Canterbury crossing spoons with a bevy of bishops and actresses; Mary Wilson and Barbara Castle mixing it with Max Bygraves and Terry Wogan; Maître Chefs (not to mention Elizabeth David) cutting capers with a hundred stars of radio, film and TV, of pitch, page, pulpit, platform and palette.

And all for SHELTER.

Probably no other cause could mount such a glittering charity show. For SHELTER is now re-housing people in Britain at the rate of ten families a day. By SHELTER's calculation there are still a million families in need of homes . . . and that calls for funds.

What better method of raising them than a kitchen frolic, in which Jeremy Thorpe forgoes his rights and the Earl of Harewood his royalties, all for the cause?

Just read the Contents List again. Surely you're not going to have it said you can't do as well as that lot. So buy a copy and contribute your mite.